Protecting Human Rights

ISSUES

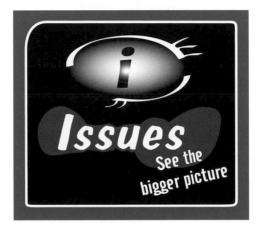

Volume 229

Series Editor

Lisa Firth

Independence

Educational Publishers

First published by Independence

The Studio, High Green

Great Shelford

Cambridge CB22 5EG

England

© Independence 2012

British Library Cataloguing in Publication Data

Protecting human rights. -- (Issues ; v. 229)

1. Human rights--Great Britain.

I. Series II. Firth, Lisa.

323'.0941-dc23

ISBN-13: 978 1 86168 618 3

Printed in Great Britain

MWL Print Group Ltd

CONTENTS

Chapter 1 Human Rights Issues

Chapter 2 Minority Rights

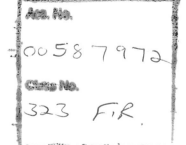

OTHER TITLES IN THE ISSUES SERIES

For more on these titles, visit: www.independence.co.uk

A note on critical evaluation

Because the information reprinted here is from a number of different sources, readers should bear in mind the origin of the text and whether the source is likely to have a particular bias when presenting information (just as they would if undertaking their own research). It is hoped that, as you read about the many aspects of the issues explored in this book, you will critically evaluate the information presented. It is important that you decide whether you are being presented with facts or opinions. Does the writer give a biased or an unbiased report? If an opinion is being expressed, do you agree with the writer?

Protecting Human Rights offers a useful starting point for those who need convenient access to information about the many issues involved. However, it is only a starting point. Following each article is a URL to the relevant organisation's website, which you may wish to visit for further information.

An introduction to human rights

Information from the Equality and Human Rights Commission.

What are human rights?

'Human rights' are the basic rights and freedoms that belong to every person in the world.

Ideas about human rights have evolved over many centuries. But they achieved strong international support following the Holocaust and World War II. To protect future generations from a repeat of these horrors, the United Nations adopted the Universal Declaration of Human Rights in 1948. For the first time, the Universal Declaration set out the fundamental rights and freedoms shared by all human beings.

'Human rights' are the basic rights and freedoms that belong to every person in the world

These rights and freedoms – based on core principles like dignity, equality and respect – inspired a range of international and regional human rights treaties. For example, they formed the basis for the European Convention on Human Rights in 1950. The European Convention protects the human rights of people in countries that belong to the Council of Europe. This includes the United Kingdom.

Until recently, people in the United Kingdom had to complain to the European Court of Human Rights in Strasbourg if they felt their rights under the European Convention had been breached. However, the Human Rights Act 1998 made these human rights part of our domestic law, and now courts here in the United Kingdom can hear human rights cases.

How do human rights help you?

Human rights are based on core principles like dignity, fairness, equality, respect and autonomy. They are relevant to your day-to-day life and protect your freedom to control your own life, effectively take part in decisions made by public authorities which impact upon your rights, and get fair and equal services from public authorities.

They help you to flourish and fulfil your potential through:

⇨ being safe and protected from harm;

⇨ being treated fairly and with dignity;

⇨ living the life you choose;

⇨ taking an active part in your community and wider society.

How do human rights work?

Where are your human rights set out?

The Human Rights Act 1998 sets out the rights in the UK which are protected by the European Convention on Human Rights.

The Act did not invent human rights for British people. Instead, it introduced into our domestic law some of the rights set out in the Universal Declaration of Human Rights and other international documents. More specifically, it gave greater effect within the UK to the rights and freedoms protected by the European Convention on Human Rights, a treaty which British lawyers helped to draft. So the Act meant that these basic rights and freedoms are now more easily protected within the UK.

Who does the Human Rights Act apply to?

The Act applies to all public authorities (such as central government departments, local authorities and NHS Trusts) and other bodies performing public functions (such as private companies operating prisons). These organisations must comply with the Act – and your human rights – when providing you with a service or making decisions that have a decisive impact upon your rights.

Although the Act does not apply to private individuals or companies (except where they are performing public functions), sometimes a public authority has a duty to stop people or companies abusing your human rights. For example, a public authority that knows a child is being abused by its parents has a duty to protect the child from inhuman or degrading treatment.

Who is protected by the Human Rights Act?

The Human Rights Act covers everyone in the United Kingdom, regardless of citizenship or immigration status. Anyone who is in the UK for any reason is protected by the provisions in the Human Rights Act.

After the Smith case (Secretary of State for Defence vs R and HM Assistant Deputy Coroner for Oxfordshire and Equality and Human Rights Commission), the Human Rights Act was also held to cover individuals outside of the UK if they were under British jurisdiction. This means, for example, that British soldiers serving overseas are protected by the Human Rights Act.

The Human Rights Act sets out the fundamental rights and freedoms that individuals in the UK have access to

The rights in the HRA are known as 'justicible', which means that if an individual thinks they have been breached, they can take a court case against the public sector body that has breached them.

Your human rights

The HRA sets out the fundamental rights and freedoms that individuals in the UK have access to. They include:

⇨ Right to life.

⇨ Freedom from torture and inhuman or degrading treatment.

⇨ Right to liberty and security.

⇨ Freedom from slavery and forced labour.

⇨ Right to a fair trial.

⇨ No punishment without law.

⇨ Respect for your private and family life, home and correspondence.

⇨ Freedom of thought, belief and religion.

⇨ Freedom of expression.

⇨ Freedom of assembly and association.

⇨ Right to marry and start a family.

⇨ Protection from discrimination in respect of these rights and freedoms.

⇨ Right to peaceful enjoyment of your property.

⇨ Right to education.

⇨ Right to participate in free elections.

Can human rights ever be restricted?

Some human rights – like the right not to be tortured – are absolute. These 'absolute' rights can never be interfered with by the Government in any circumstances.

However, most human rights are not absolute. Some of these rights can be limited in certain circumstances, as set out in the specified Article of the European Convention on Human Rights. For example, your right to liberty can be limited only in specified circumstances such as if you are convicted and sentenced to a prison term. Other rights can only be restricted when certain general conditions are met, for example where this is necessary to protect the rights of others or in the interests of the wider community. For example, the Government may be able to restrict your right to freedom of expression if you are encouraging racial hatred.

⇨ The above information is reprinted with kind permission from the Equality and Human Rights Commission. Visit www.equalityhumanrights.com for more information.

EQUALITY AND HUMAN RIGHTS COMMISSION

Human Rights Act myths

Information from Liberty.

There has been very little public education about the rights and freedoms contained in the Human Rights Act and how it works. As a result, many myths and misunderstandings have sprung up about the HRA – including who it does and doesn't protect and what values it contains.

Exploding these myths is a crucial part of our Common Values campaign. Here are some of the most common false accusations against the Act.

'The Human Rights Act does nothing for ordinary people'

The Human Rights Act protects everyone's human rights; young and old, rich and poor, yours and mine. Anybody's privacy could be breached by the prying eyes of the state, anybody can be wrongly accused of a crime, and anybody could fall foul of careless and insensitive decision-making by public authorities. Hopefully this won't happen to you but if it did, you might find you need to rely on the Human Rights Act to help you.

'People now have a "human right" to anything'

The Human Rights Act doesn't protect an endless catalogue of rights. Indeed, it only protects 15 well-established fundamental rights and freedoms, like the right to life and free speech. Unfortunately, however, myths abound about claims that have been upheld using the Act.

Many other democracies protect a far broader range of rights. In fact, the rights contained in the Human Rights Act are so fundamental that no other modern democracy has scrapped their equivalent human rights legislation. Just as the USA would not scrap its Bill of Rights, we should not scrap ours.

'The HRA is a charter for criminals and terrorists – it does nothing for victims'

The HRA protects the rights of everyone. The protection of victims of crime and human rights abuses lies at the heart of human rights law. Indeed, many of the rights protected under the HRA can be limited in the interests of public safety, in order to protect national security or to prevent an offence being committed. The Human Rights Act also puts positive obligations on the State to protect victims. The HRA requires serious offences like murder, terrorism and rape to be investigated by the police, and requires the State to take practical steps to protect people whose rights are threatened by others. The Act specifically states that those suspected of or convicted of crimes can be deprived of their liberty. Human rights law has given bereaved relatives the right to an independent public investigation into the circumstances surrounding the death of their loved ones, and the right to be involved in the investigation.

'The Human Rights Act has made us all less safe. It needs amending so that the courts are required to balance our rights to safety and security'

The Human Rights Act already requires the courts to balance human rights against the interests of public safety. There are some rights that are absolute and can never be limited, for example the right not to be tortured or enslaved. However, most of our rights and freedoms can be limited where necessary and proportionate. For example, the Act allows the right to freedom, speech, protest and privacy to be restricted where this is necessary to protect public safety or national security. The Act specifically says those suspected of or convicted of crimes can be deprived of their liberty. Human rights law also requires the State to protect our safety and security.

Human rights legislation was drafted after the horrors of the Second World War. Thankfully, countries like the UK that have remained committed to protecting human rights have not seen a repeat of such atrocities. Sadly, war and civil unrest is still rife in countries where human rights violations remain a tragic reality. We cannot call for an end to rights abuses elsewhere in the world unless we show a commitment to protecting rights at home as well.

'The Human Rights Act has cost the British taxpayer millions of pounds and has been a goldmine for lawyers'

One of the main reasons for the Act was the cost and delay caused by the fact that people could only enforce their human rights by taking cases to a court in Strasbourg. People's rights can now be protected by British courts, which is far more efficient and cost-effective. But the Human Rights Act is not just about lawyers and courts. It has helped thousands of people protect their human rights without the need for costly court cases. Local authorities have reviewed their policies to make sure they treat the vulnerable with dignity and respect and users of a wide range of public services have used the Act as a tool to argue for better and fairer services.

'The HRA has been imposed on us by the EU'

The HRA was independently passed by the UK Parliament in 1998. It incorporates the Convention for the Protection of Human Rights and Fundamental Freedoms. The Convention was adopted by the Council of Europe in 1950 – a body set up after WWII to promote democracy, human rights and the rule of law in Europe. This body is completely separate to the EU. The UK played a major role in the negotiations and drafting of the Convention, which it voluntarily adopted in 1951.

'British common law and the Magna Carta protected our rights long before the HRA'

The UK has a long and proud history in leading the development and recognition of fundamental rights and freedoms. In fact, many of the rights in the HRA had their genesis in principles that emerged from the Magna Carta, the 1689 Bill of Rights, the Habeas Corpus Acts and the common law. However, the common law is liable to be overridden at any time by statute and provides no possible recourse when rights are undermined. There is also nothing in Magna Carta or other historic legislation that protects free speech, personal privacy, the right to protest, non-discrimination etc. Many of the rights

we have long taken for granted found no protection in domestic law until the HRA gave effect to them. Until the advent of the HRA, British residents had to rely solely on the good will of government for protection or take the long and costly route to the European Court of Human Rights. While the freedom of a person to do anything that is not prohibited by law is an important part of our constitution, this principle gives no protection to individuals from misuse of power by the state or public bodies.

'The HRA gives too much power to unelected judges'

Unlike most Bills of Rights and constitutional documents around the world, the HRA does not give the courts any power to strike down legislation. Rather, it adopts a compromise – maintaining parliamentary sovereignty and setting up a dialogue model between the courts and Parliament. Under the HRA, if one of the higher courts finds legislation to be incompatible with human rights it can issue a declaration of incompatibility, leaving it up to Parliament to decide how best to respond. One of the cornerstones of our democratic system is an independent judiciary that interprets and applies the law. Judicial decision-making is fundamental to the rule of law, and the powers given by the HRA to the courts fall squarely within this historic function.

'The HRA is all about rights and not about responsibilities'

Human rights and responsibilities are inextricably bound together. Rights mean little if others do not take responsibility to protect them. And most rights are not absolute – instead they can be limited if necessary to protect the rights of others. So, for example, the right to free speech explicitly carries with it duties and responsibilities, such as not to incite violence or wilfully defame others. The HRA also explicitly states that none of the rights can be interpreted as implying that anyone has the right to intentionally destroy other people's human rights or limit them more than is allowable under the HRA. While many rights come with responsibilities, rights are also universal and inalienable in nature. Self-evidently a person could not, for example, be denied a right to a fair trial because they are suspected of having committed a crime.

'The HRA prevents us from deporting foreigners'

There is no general prohibition in the HRA on the deportation of non-nationals. If the Government decides that a citizen of another country who has limited ties to the UK should no longer be permitted to stay and can be safely sent back to their country of origin there

is nothing in the HRA to prevent this. However, under international human rights law the absolute prohibition on torture prevents countries from sending a person anywhere where there is a substantial risk that the person will be tortured. This is entirely logical. If we abhor torture we must also abhor the outsourcing of torture – if governments were only prohibited from torturing their own citizens but permitted to send people to places of torture, there would be little distinction between deportation and extraordinary rendition. Even before the HRA was enacted the Convention Against Torture, the European Convention on Human Rights and the International Convention on Civil and Political Rights prohibited the UK from deporting people to places of torture.

Depending on the facts of each individual case, a person's right to a family life may be interfered with in some cases if deported. Home Office policy is to consider the facts of each case, including the reason for the deportation (i.e. whether a serious or minor offence has been committed), the length of time the person has been in the UK and whether the person has young children born in the UK or a British spouse, etc. This is the type of balancing exercise that would as a matter of policy be carried out by the Home Office regardless of the HRA, but the HRA has provided greater transparency, accountability and oversight of Home Office decisions in this area.

'Prisoners have the right to access hardcore pornography because of human rights'

In 2001 there were numerous media reports that the serial killer Dennis Nilsen was using human rights law to demand access to hardcore pornography in prison. Since then it has been widely reported that human rights law gives prisoners access to hardcore pornography. However, while Dennis Nilsen tried to claim he was entitled to hardcore pornography under human rights law, the court denied him permission even to bring the claim, on the basis there was no arguable case that his human rights had been breached.

'Police can't put up "Wanted" posters of dangerous criminals on the run because of their human rights'

Since 2007 there have been reports that police are unable to release photographs of dangerous criminals on the run because this would breach their human rights. However, the HRA itself protects the right to life and imposes an obligation on the State to protect people from serious criminal attack. In some circumstances the Government may actually be duty-bound under human rights law to publicise photographs of dangerous

convicted criminals if this would protect others. The right to privacy can be limited for the protection and detection of crime as long as it is necessary and proportionate to do so – seeking to locate dangerous criminals and warn the public is certainly not a breach of human rights law.

'Police gave fried chicken to a burglar because of his "human rights"'

In 2006 a suspected car thief fleeing police was besieged on a roof for 20 hours. During the course of the 20-hour stand-off, the police negotiating team gave the man Kentucky Fried Chicken and cigarettes. It was widely reported that the police did this in order to protect the man's 'wellbeing and human rights'. There was clearly no human right engaged – there is no human right to KFC, nor indeed to be provided with any food in such a situation. Rather, the police were using general negotiating tactics to encourage him to come down from the roof.

'The right to privacy in the HRA prevents free media reporting'

The HRA protects both the right to privacy and the right to free expression. At times these rights can come into conflict with one another and when they do a balancing exercise is required. The HRA has on many occasions strengthened the free press. In particular the right to free speech (enshrined in Article 10) will protect media reports that are of public concern and in the public interest. Indeed, the right to free speech finds its only protection in UK law under Article 10 of the HRA. Article 10 has protected journalists from being required to disclose their sources and has provided protection of investigative reporting. However, it will not protect reports that are obviously false and may not protect intrusive reports relating to the private lives of individuals. In some cases the right to privacy, in conjunction with the common law, will prevent media reports into the private lives of celebrities when it is not in the public interest to report such private details.

'The HRA has created a compensation culture'

The remedies available under the HRA are focused on bringing any infringement of human rights to an end. A claim based on breach of human rights is not the same as a case brought under the law of negligence, where the purpose of the claim is to obtain damages. In human rights claims, compensation is a secondary consideration and often not awarded at all. The HRA provides that compensation can only be awarded once all the circumstances of the case are taken into account, including what other relief is available. There

is no right to compensation – it is only awarded when it is necessary to ensure 'just satisfaction'. The courts will also consider the behaviour of an applicant before awarding damages. Very few human rights cases involve awards of damages.

'Because of the HRA public bodies are frightened of making the wrong decision and criminals end up being released early'

In November 2004, sex offender Anthony Rice was released from prison on parole after having served 16 years of a life sentence for a violent attempted rape. He had previous convictions for rape and indecent assault. In August 2005 he raped and murdered Naomi Bryant while on release on licence. The following year a review carried out in relation to the Parole Board's decision to release concluded that part of the reason for the early release was based on a misunderstanding of human rights considerations. Following this it was widely reported that Rice was freed 'because of his human rights'. In reality, there is no evidence the Parole Board even considered human rights. Rice was freed because of a series of mistakes, including that relevant information about Rice's past crimes – which included a serious assault on a five-year-old – was not made available to the Parole Board.

The right to privacy under Article 8 of the HRA can be limited if it is necessary and proportionate to protect public safety

---

The Joint Committee on Human Rights has concluded that Rice was not released because of human rights considerations – a finding that the author of the 2006 review has himself endorsed. There is no human rights objection to continued incarceration of a convicted dangerous offender who had not yet served his full sentence. In fact, the right to life under Article 2 of the HRA requires the State to take steps to protect life. It is because of the right to life that Naomi Bryant's mother has been able to secure an inquest into the circumstances leading to the death of her daughter. There is no evidence that any criminal has been released from prison early on the mistaken belief that this was required by the HRA.

'The HRA prevents rapists and paedophiles from registering their details on the sex offenders register'

There is nothing in the HRA that prevents convicted sex offenders from being required to register on the sex offenders register. The right to privacy under

Article 8 of the HRA can be limited if it is necessary and proportionate to protect public safety. The courts have held that registration on the sex offenders register does not breach human rights law. In 2010 it was, however, wrongly reported that plans to require sex offenders to disclose email addresses and online identities (for example, on Facebook) had been shelved because it would breach offenders' human rights. Instead the European Court of Human Rights has held that the requirement to provide information to the police for inclusion on the sex offenders register is proportionate given the gravity of the harm which may be caused to the victims of sexual offences if an offender were to reoffend.

Our Supreme Court has held that while life-long registration on the register can be justified, there should be a mechanism to provide simply for a review of the requirement to remain on the register long-term. A review would consider an individual's circumstances and may well lead to a decision to continue to require registration.

'The HRA is not sufficiently "British" so the UK doesn't benefit from the "margin of appreciation" before the European Court of Human Rights'

The European Court of Human Rights (ECtHR) gives a margin of appreciation to member states to allow for political and cultural variations between the 47 different countries that have signed up to the Convention on Human Rights. It will also be applied where the ECtHR considers national authorities are better placed to make assessments of proportionality about rights protection.

How much emphasis is placed on the margin of appreciation will depend on the nature of the human right at issue (for example, religious freedom might attract the principle whereas torture will not); the reason why the State has limited the right; and whether there are differing approaches to the issue within member states or if a country is alone in limiting the right in that way. Some commentators have suggested that only a clear and codified 'British Bill of Rights' would lead the ECtHR to give the UK the benefit of our home-grown values – that it requires a constitutional document like the German Basic Law before the ECtHR will defer to domestic practice. This is not how the margin of appreciation has been applied by the ECtHR (the margin of appreciation is solely an international doctrine and is not available to UK courts). The adoption of a differently-named 'British Bill of Rights', or indeed a written constitution, would have no added effect in ensuring the ECtHR applied a greater margin of appreciation to the UK.

⇨ Information from Liberty. Visit www.liberty-human-rights.org.uk for more.

© Liberty

Should we repeal the Human Rights Act?

With discussions ongoing about the need for a British Bill of Rights, Bill Cash and Julian Huppert disagree on whether the UK's current legislation should be replaced.

Bill Cash MP (Conservative) says yes

When I was Shadow Attorney General, I recommended – and my party accepted – that we repeal the Human Rights Act (HRA) 1998. The Act does not protect British people from harm, let alone their liberties. It should also not be up to unelected judges to decide on what amounts to policy matters in the British national interest. My view of repeal was instituted as Conservative Party policy, which continued through to the last election.

The Conservative manifesto, on which all Conservative MPs campaigned at the 2010 general election, stated: 'To protect our freedoms from state encroachment and encourage greater social responsibility, we will replace the Human Rights Act with a UK Bill of Rights.' The Prime Minister himself repeatedly said that he thoroughly endorsed the pledge.

The replacement of the HRA was then relegated to a review under the Coalition agreement. Nick Clegg reversed the real Conservative position: the HRA will not be repealed, and there will be no proper reform of our position towards the Act, which incorporated the European Convention on Human Rights (ECHR) into UK law.

Nick Clegg had already got his way when the Coalition agreement stated: 'We will establish a commission to investigate the creation of a British Bill of Rights that incorporates and builds on all our obligations under the European Convention on Human Rights, ensures that these rights continue to be enshrined in British law, and protects and extends British liberties. We will seek to promote a better understanding of the true scope of these obligations and liberties.'

The Bill of Rights Commission has now been created, and has lost credibility because many of its members overtly support the whole structure of the ECHR and the HRA. These include Lord Lester, a QC who campaigned for 30 years for the ECHR to be incorporated in British law, and also Labour peer and human rights lawyer Baroness Kennedy. Although a few members have not been totally absorbed into the human rights legislation DNA, the commission seriously lacks balance. In short, the current position is that the Coalition Government is unwilling to deal with the Act, and failing to deal with the ECHR.

Last year, over 300 foreign prisoners – including killers – successfully avoided deportation by the Home Office after claiming they have a human right to a 'family life' in Britain, under Article 8 of the HRA. The sloppy wording of the outdated Convention, as understood through the Act, has led to the gagging of the press, gagging of freedom of speech and interference in privacy law, among other difficulties.

The HRA undermines the best traditions of British freedoms. British constitutional history is being written out as the Convention is enforced, and we must seek to protect our Parliament if we are not going to allow our constitution to become extinct.

In dealing with terrorists, we had control orders and counter-terrorist measures that failed, because we had bound our Parliament under the terms of the HRA and the ECHR. I have proposed a Prevention of Terrorism Bill, which would unwind the application of the Act and give us a proper terrorism law, ruling out the application of the HRA 1998 while insisting on *habeas corpus*, due process and fair trial on one hand, and guiding judicial interpretation of provisions during a public emergency on the other. In the meantime, the British people will be governed under the ineffective, flawed anti-terror legislation devised under the terms of the HRA.

To govern the British people on our own terms, we must repeal the Act. As I said in a debate in Westminster

Hall recently, I am all for a Bill of Rights, but which one? Similarly, on the question of the rule of law: which law, whose law, and who is going to enforce it? Whatever emerges must have unimpeachable superior jurisdiction, based on Westminster overriding any other competing jurisdiction on behalf of the British people. We must have British law for British judges if we are truly to defend and govern the British people.

Bill Cash is the Conservative MP for Stone and chairman of the European Scrutiny Committee in the Commons.

Julian Huppert MP (Liberal Democrat) says No

I have a poster on my office door that lists the rights enshrined in the Human Rights Act – in the shape of a heart. Underneath the heart, the poster asks: 'What's not to love?'

It is a clear way of summing up the problem at the heart of the 'debate' on the HRA. Since its introduction in 1998 – a long-held Liberal/Liberal Democrat policy finally implemented – the amount of misinformation peddled about the Act has attained ludicrous proportions. People hold misconceptions, and then base their view of the Act upon them. The right-wing press, in particular, actively fuels these misconceptions.

One notorious example was the Dennis Nilsen case. In 2001, numerous media reports said that Nilsen was using human rights law to demand access in prison to hardcore pornography. It has since become a well-known meme among those who oppose the HRA to suggest that human rights law gave prisoners access to hardcore porn. In reality, the court denied Nilsen even permission to bring a claim, as there was no arguable case that any of his human rights were being breached. However, this is rarely pointed out.

It's an insidious problem, as those who want to jettison this vital piece of legislation are given free rein to build convincing-sounding strawmen. And, by the same token, they can avoid explaining which of the rights they object to. Is it the right to life? The right to freedom of thought, religion and belief? The right to free elections? Or even the freedom of assembly?

The rights enshrined in the HRA come from the European Convention on Human Rights (ECHR). This, in itself, creates further confusion, as many people hear the word 'European' and assume, falsely, that it refers to the European Union and is part of an EU project to change the British way of life.

In fact, the ECHR was proposed and negotiated for strongly by the UK, drafted mainly by British lawyers and adopted by the Council of Europe (a council first proposed by Winston Churchill during World War II and established in 1949). As Jesse Norman and Peter Oborne have noted in their pamphlet *Churchill's Legacy: The Conservative Case for the Human Rights Act*, the ECHR stands as a formidable political achievement, and it would send a terrible message both to our European allies and to the world if we withdrew from it. The ECHR was, largely, Britain's statement of principles, and a challenge to the rest of Europe to match us. It would be a disgrace to fail our own challenge.

The chief argument used to introduce the Act wasn't based on the proud British principles that many of us would have liked; it was a practical and pragmatic piece of legislation designed to avoid costly trips to Strasbourg every time someone wanted to challenge a law that they perceived was infringing their rights. Repealing the Act would reinstate that expense, and result in more decisions about Britain being made in Strasbourg, rather than by our own judges.

The error made with the Act was in failing afterwards to explain its benefits. The Labour Government that introduced it found itself competing with it on too many occasions, as it embarked upon a major attack against our civil liberties through a programme of centralised authoritarianism, done in the name of 'the war on terror'. What good was the HRA when New Labour's database state was being built, tourists, photographers and trainspotters were routinely treated as terrorist suspects, and the right to peaceful protest was systematically eroded until it became almost a cipher?

We must be clear, however, on what the Act is not. It is not a Bill of Rights in the style of the American constitution, with the power to strike down legislation that does not comply. In that sense, it does not go far enough for those who'd like the judiciary to act as a greater balance against governments afflicted by legislative diarrhoea. But the HRA has, nonetheless, had an important impact on the political discourse in our country – it has acted as a totemic reminder of the need to strike a balance between liberty and security, and to preserve the liberties that grew up naturally as a result of our common law.

I'm delighted that my party stands in the way of the Conservatives' calls for repeal. Such an action would be legally impotent, and – more importantly – would deeply damage our common values.

Julian Huppert is the Liberal Democrat MP for Cambridge, and a member of the Home Affairs Select Committee and the Joint Committee on Human Rights.

13 June 2011

⇨ This article originally appeared in *Total Politics* magazine. Visit www.totalpolitics.com/subscribe to get your copy.

© *Total Politics*

UK bill of rights commission should open up

Government panel examining human rights law should be courting public attention, not avoiding it.

By Adam Wagner

Things have been quiet recently on the Commission on a Bill of Rights front, with media attention focused on the upcoming Brighton conference on European Court of Human Rights reform and the growing controversy over the justice and security green paper. But this important commission only has ten months left to publish its report, and it should be courting public attention, not avoiding it.

There has been limited action on the commission's website, with publication of relatively illuminating minutes from the 15 November and 14 December meetings. The website has also published a list of all responses to the recent consultation. Apparently there were over 900 responses to the somewhat scanty discussion paper which was published last year.

Two suggestions. First, in my view, all of the responses should be published on the commission's website, not just a list of the respondees. I asked the commission by email whether they would be doing so, and they responded:

'We will of course be including analyses of the discussion paper responses in our final report. Until that time and given that the commission has such a small secretariat, we do not currently have any plans to publish an analysis of the responses ahead of the final report.'

I take the point on resources, but this commission's task is one of fundamental importance to the UK public and as such should operate in as open and transparent a way as possible. If there is not enough money for it to do so, then it should ask for more. The Justice and Security Green Paper consultation has published its responses online and even linked to other web resources, including this blog. *The Guardian* reported on Sunday this comment from the Cabinet Office:

'In the interests of ensuring maximum transparency, we are actively seeking consent to publish as many responses as possible. Even in cases where consent is withheld we are proposing to publish a summary that reflects the full range of responses received. Separately, a very small number of responses were submitted in confidence. The government is under a legal duty to respect that.'

The same logic should apply to the Commission on a Bill of Rights. If the somewhat airbrushed minutes are anything to go by – there is no mention of who said what, only that a debate was held on an issue – we will have no way of knowing once the report is published how it links to the views expressed in the consultation responses, except in vague terms.

My second suggestion, again given the importance of its task to the public, is that the commission should launch a proper public consultation in good time before it has to report. This is hinted at in the December 2011 minutes ([the Secretary] noted that he had spoken to Ben Page, Chief Executive of Ipsos MORI, to discuss possible options for consulting the public and that he hoped to be able to circulate a proposal from Mr Page to members shortly); it should happen and time is running out for a proper consultation to be held and considered. 900 responses is a poor show for a commission which could affect the public's basic rights for a generation and no recommendations should be made without hearing what the general public thinks.

One of the commission's tasks is to 'consider ways to promote a better understanding of the true scope of these obligations and liberties'. This is especially important in light of the often-heard criticism of the Human Rights Act that the public do not feel they 'own' it. Indeed, this was the main justification for the commission in the first place.

You only need to open up a newspaper to find a fierce and heated debate going on about human rights in the UK. This sometimes generates more heat than light, but the public is clearly engaged at some level. It is bizarre that the Commission on a Bill of Rights, which was set up to resolve that debate, is the only remaining 'public' space where there is little evidence of any kind of passionate argument over human rights going on.

I suspect that the instinct of the chair – former permanent secretary Sir Leigh Lewis – is publicly to paper over disagreements rather than exposing squabbles within the commission (e.g. the odd 'side letter' which was published early on). This must be the wrong approach.

The commission should not see the lack of public attention as an opportunity to get on with its work in peace. Rather, it should see public apathy as a fundamental threat to its task. It should therefore be seeking out attention in creative ways, including the use of the Internet and wide ranging public consultation. Only this will ensure that the commission's important work is open, transparent and ultimately successful.

5 March 2012

THE GUARDIAN

New snooping powers could be illegal, human rights watchdog warns

New powers to snoop on every email, web visit and phone call could be illegal due to breaching privacy laws, the human rights watchdog warned yesterday.

By Tom Whitehead

The sheer scale of the Government plans to allow police and security agencies access to every communication by every citizen may be an unlawful invasion of the right to privacy, according to the Equality and Human Rights Commission (EHRC).

The warning came as a former police leader said the plan, which will cost the public £200 million a year, was 'fraught with danger' and a 'massive state intervention' into people's lives.

Sir Chris Fox, the former president of the Association of Chief Police Officers (ACPO), said the proposals were 'not appropriate in a free country'.

The Coalition is facing an intense backlash over plans to force communications providers to record and store every activity of their customers for at least a year.

It is to allow police and intelligence officers to monitor who someone is in contact with and the websites they visit, although the content of communications will not be accessed.

Local councils and other government agencies, such as those investigating benefit fraud, may also be able to get the information.

But the EHRC warned the move is not proportionate and is likely to breach the European Convention on Human Rights, which gives an individual a right to privacy.

It also believes human rights laws will be breached because members of the public will not be able to have an effective right of redress if they are inappropriately or wrongly targeted.

The Information Commissioner's Office yesterday warned that the nature of communication technology increased the risk of someone being the victim of mistaken identity.

But the EHRC said the sheer numbers potentially involved – the entire population – would make any redress system almost impossible to work effectively.

Trevor Phillips, chairman of the EHRC, said: 'We do understand that there is a balance between safety and security, but this proposal looks like overkill.

'It sounds like building a monstrous haystack to find a needle which may or may not exist.

'It would ultimately be for the Supreme Court to decide, but to be consistent with the right to privacy the legislation would need to incorporate effective remedies against abuse.

'The Commission's research on information privacy shows that the current regulatory system is struggling to cope and it is hard to see how this proposal would do anything other than make it harder for people to protect their own privacy.'

The plan ... will cost the public £200 million a year

The Home Office argues the powers are necessary to help the police and security services keep ahead of terrorists and criminals who exploit new communications technology.

But Sir Chris Fox, who as ACPO president in 2005 helped coordinate the police response in the wake of the 7/7 terror attacks in London, attacked the proposals as 'fraught with danger for the innocent vast majority'.

He told BBC Radio 4: 'It just seems to me to be inappropriate. A massive intervention by the state into private lives.

'It is not appropriate in a free country. Are the terrorists forcing us to be a controlled and invasive society?'

ACPO itself was less critical yesterday but said any changes must be 'justified and proportionate'.

Assistant Chief Constable Gary Beautridge, the spokesman on data communications, said: 'The impact of communications data on serious criminal investigations should not be underestimated: it is critical to the ability of the police service to protect the public.

'Telecommunications technology is changing rapidly and in this new world there is a need to look at how we can ensure the capability to investigate crime, save lives and prosecute offenders is maintained.

'It is a matter for government to ensure the right boundaries are set so that our approaches are justified, necessary and proportionate.'

4 April 2012

© Telegraph Media Group Limited 2012

THE TELEGRAPH

Global increase in human rights violations

Arab Spring uprisings, African 'land grabs' and the economic downturn causing global increase in human rights violations, reveals Maplecroft 'Risk Atlas'.

An annual *Human Rights Risk Atlas (HRRA)*, analysing the extent of human rights abuses in 197 countries, has revealed that human rights and labour standards risks for companies and investors are increasing on a global scale, with 48% of the world now posing 'extreme' or 'high' risks of corporate complicity in rights violations.

According to risk analysis and mapping company Maplecroft, author of the fifth annual *HRRA*, citizens in 95 countries are now exposed to human rights violations by states. This represents a 6% increase in countries posing 'extreme' or 'high' risks to business and investors since 2010.

Maplecroft states that the global increase in human rights risk is attributed, in part, to three main factors. First, the violent crackdown on protesters by security forces during the Arab Spring uprisings, which were sparked by anti-government sentiments relating to corruption, oppression of rights and rising food prices. Second, an emerging set of resource-scarcity challenges for business, linked to large scale 'land grabs' in developing countries by foreign investors aimed at increasing food, water and energy security at home, including biofuels production. In addition, the global economic recession continued to challenge the rights of workers, with the results of the *HRRA* revealing a trend for the trafficking of migrant workers for forced labour in countries such as Malaysia, Russia, South Africa and UAE.

The *HRRA 2012* has been developed by Maplecroft to enable organisations to evaluate and monitor the risks and responsibilities of investing in countries and companies in terms of their human rights risk exposures in their global operations, investments or supply chains. It analyses 23 types of human rights violation within the categories of human security, labour rights, civil and political rights and access to remedy.

Arab Spring exposes risks of complicity with state security forces for the energy sector

While the Arab Spring protests aimed to boost the protection of human rights, they led to a surge of violations due to high levels of violence by security forces against opposition groups and protesters. In almost all Middle East and North Africa (MENA) countries, the risk of human rights violations increased in the *HRRA* over the last year. In the 'extreme risk' category, Yemen (8th), Iraq (9th) and Iran (10th) saw slight increases in

the rankings, while Libya (26th) and Syria (13th) rose 25 and 14 places respectively, indicating a significant rise in risk. The states of Egypt (35th) and Bahrain (42nd), both rated 'high risk,' climbed 11 and 60 places respectively and now sit just outside the highest risk category.

Complicity with the actions of the states in MENA countries pose significant risks to investors in the energy sector, which has extensive interests in the oil- and gas-rich region. A particular risk for companies is complicity with the actions of state and private security forces. Both are used in the protection of company operations, and assets and associations with their actions in the repression of rights can result in significant reputational damage and legal risks. The excessive and lethal force used by state security in these countries, such as the ongoing killings of civilians in Syria and Egypt, as well as attacks on civil and political rights, highlights these risks vividly.

According to a May 2011 report in The Guardian, half of the 3.2 million hectares of biofuel land identified in Africa is linked to 11 British companies: more than any other country

A further factor in the worsening situation in MENA countries is enhanced digital inclusion, where the rise of social media and digital photography has exponentially improved the reporting of human rights violations.

Companies must integrate ESG factors into investment analysis

Maplecroft states that companies investing in emerging economies benefit from high growth rates and contribute significantly to development. However, due to long-term structural risks in these countries, such as their human rights environment, they are at increased social risk. Therefore to maximise opportunity and minimise risk, they need to assess potential negative human rights' impacts, prevent them where possible and engage with partners to promote responsible investment.

'In the face of a deteriorating human rights situation, corporations can expect increased scrutiny from stakeholders and investors, making it imperative for them

MAPLECROFT

to assess, mitigate, manage and monitor these risks,' states Maplecroft CEO Alyson Warhurst. 'It is becoming critical for organisations to integrate environmental, social and governance factors, such as human rights impact assessment, into their decision-making, or they leave themselves exposed to reputational damage, legal actions and costs to the business that in turn might lead to requirements to divest.'

Land grabs impact rights of the most vulnerable rural populations

The *HRRA 2012* also finds that a rising trend for large-scale land acquisitions, or 'land grabs,' by foreign investors, especially in Africa, is increasingly impacting the human rights of the most vulnerable populations. The right of local communities to water, food and adequate housing, and the right to gain a living, can all be adversely affected by such investments unless significant measures are taken to ensure their protection. Indigenous peoples are at particular risk, as their land rights are often not safeguarded.

States such as China, India, South Korea and the Gulf States are buying up land in developing countries to grow crops abroad, while private energy companies based in the UK, Germany and Sweden are securing land in sub-Saharan Africa for the production of biofuels. According to a May 2011 report in *The Guardian*, half of the 3.2 million hectares of biofuel land identified in Africa is linked to 11 British companies: more than any other country.

Sub-Saharan African countries that have undertaken large-scale land deals with foreign investors include DR Congo, Ethiopia, Mozambique, Mali, Sudan and Tanzania, all of which are classified as 'extreme' or 'high risk' in the *HRRA*. In Sudan, over the last year alone, companies from South Korea and UAE purchased 1.5 million hectares of agricultural land between them. It is also reported that some investors have been given unrestricted access to water in the country, a move that could negatively impact the livelihoods of local Sudanese.

Deals such as these illustrate the cross-cutting links between environmental, social and governance risks that create a range of ethical business dilemmas for investors in the agri-commodities sector, including human rights, deforestation and the loss of biodiversity. 'The debate around global food and water security in fragile and conflict-affected countries in relation to human rights has intensified,' continues Warhurst. 'To avoid financial and reputational damage, investors in such projects should ensure they contain safeguards that also benefit the rural poor by generating employment in the sector, by developing rural infrastructure, as well as by contributing to poverty reduction.'

7 December 2011

⇨ The above information is reproduced with kind permission from Maplecroft. Please visit www.maplecroft.com for further information.

© Maplecroft

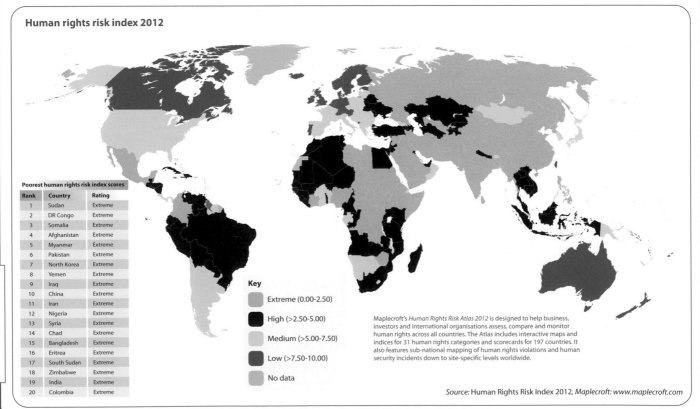

Human rights risk index 2012

Poorest human rights risk index scores

Rank	Country	Rating
1	Sudan	Extreme
2	DR Congo	Extreme
3	Somalia	Extreme
4	Afghanistan	Extreme
5	Myanmar	Extreme
6	Pakistan	Extreme
7	North Korea	Extreme
8	Yemen	Extreme
9	Iraq	Extreme
10	China	Extreme
11	Iran	Extreme
12	Nigeria	Extreme
13	Syria	Extreme
14	Chad	Extreme
15	Bangladesh	Extreme
16	Eritrea	Extreme
17	South Sudan	Extreme
18	Zimbabwe	Extreme
19	India	Extreme
20	Colombia	Extreme

Key

Extreme (0.00-2.50)

High (>2.50-5.00)

Medium (>5.00-7.50)

Low (>7.50-10.00)

No data

Maplecroft's *Human Rights Risk Atlas 2012* is designed to help business, investors and international organisations assess, compare and monitor human rights across all countries. The Atlas includes interactive maps and indices for 31 human rights categories and scorecards for 197 countries. It also features sub-national mapping of human rights violations and human security incidents down to site-specific levels worldwide.

Source: Human Rights Risk Index 2012, *Maplecroft: www.maplecroft.com*

Let's clean up fashion 2011

The state of pay behind the UK high street.

By Anna McMullen and Sam Maher

The boss says i'm very lucky to be working on some of the world's leading fashion labels!

In a global economy still reeling from the near-collapse of the banks, it is often those least able who are asked to pay the cost. The fashion industry is a prime example of this trend.

As many UK high street retailers continue to post increased profits, the real value of wages being paid to the millions of women and men employed in the industry is falling. This means that many struggle to feed, clothe and shelter their families. The state of affairs is all the more sobering because the majority of these retailers have committed to a living wage for workers in their supply chain. In fact, many have been running projects to this end for several years but, as the real situation on the ground shows, these commitments are not delivering results fast enough.

Many brands and retailers argue that the only way to reverse this trend is for governments to make sure that minimum wages more accurately reflect the needs of their citizens. We agree. Yet the very way in which the garment industry works makes this difficult. As brands and retailers constantly move from supplier to supplier in their search for ever lower prices, governments and workers are told that raising wages (and therefore costs) would scare away export business and put paid to employment and revenues.

This is why it is vital that brands and retailers commit to pay a price to their suppliers that is enough to provide a living wage to all workers. By doing this, companies can give a clear message that human rights have an importance that goes beyond profit. This could put a brake on the race to the bottom that causes the poverty characterising this industry.

Some brands have told us that, in their opinion, a living wage must be defined by workers themselves. Again, we agree. So do many workers. In the two years since this report was last released, mass demonstrations and strikes have taken place across the world, each calling on governments and employers to dramatically increase legal minimum wages. In the summer of 2010, thousands of garment workers in Bangladesh took to the streets demanding a minimum wage of 5000tk. In September 2010, workers across Cambodia took part in a national strike to demand that their wage was raised to $93 per month. And in August this year, four garment worker unions in Lesotho demonstrated to demand that the minimum wage for garment workers was increased to R2020 per month, claiming such an increase was necessary for garment workers to escape the squalor and poverty in which most are forced to live.

What was the result of these actions? In Bangladesh and Cambodia the unions won small concessions, but failed to get the wages they were demanding; wages that even if they were paid would still fail to provide a living wage. In Lesotho, negotiations were continuing at the time of writing. This came at a heavy cost. Hundreds of Bangladeshi workers and trade union leaders were arrested and a number of them are still on trial and face the prospect of years in prison. Hundreds of Cambodian workers were dismissed from their jobs – although many have since been reinstated, others face a future without work. In Lesotho, crowds gathering on the street during a three-day action were fired at by police, with several injured. Six trade union leaders were arrested and beaten. The fact is that workers do speak out to demand better wages. At best, they are often ignored; at worst they are persecuted, threatened, dismissed or harassed. Companies must do more to ensure respect for trade union rights in the quest to provide a living wage for garment workers. While these rights continue to be violated by governments, employers and brands, workers will be silenced and left open to ever worsening exploitation.

In 2011, a living wage for the garment industry is still a distant dream for the millions of workers producing our clothes. It's time for brands and retailers to stop talking and start acting on the issues that really matter.

September 2011

⇨ The above information is an extract from Labour Behind the Label's report *Let's Clean Up Fashion 2011*, and is reprinted with permission. Visit www. labourbehindthelabel.org for more information.

LABOUR BEHIND THE LABEL

All workers have rights

Information from the Irish Congress of Trade Unions.

Today's globalisation is not providing the resources needed for living and working conditions to improve for the mass of the world's people. Rather, governments are all too often undermining workers' rights and conditions so that business can minimise its labour costs. Yet all workers have rights, as has been repeatedly agreed by the same governments over the past half a century. Four decades after signing the United Nations Universal Declaration of Human Rights, governments at the World Summit for Social Development in Copenhagen in 1995 again committed themselves to:

'safeguarding and promoting respect for basic workers' rights, including the right to organise and bargain collectively; the prohibition of forced and child labour; equal remuneration for men and women for work of equal value, and non-discrimination in employment.'

International Labour Organization

The body of the United Nations which oversees labour issues is the International Labour Organization (ILO), based in Geneva, Switzerland. The ILO is the only international body that is tripartite, having representatives of governments, employers and workers. They come from 182 countries. At the ILO, the Irish Congress of Trade Unions (ICTU) represents workers on the island of Ireland.

One of the ILO's most important functions is the development of international labour standards. The ILO agrees Conventions which aim to create binding obligations on governments, and Recommendations which give guidance to governments on policy, legislation and practice.

There are over 180 ILO Conventions and even more Recommendations. As well as basic trade union rights and freedom from harassment, coercion and discrimination, they cover many issues such as safe and healthy workplaces, hours of work, paid leave for agricultural workers, contracts of employment for seafarers, etc.

Establishing standards is one thing. Making sure they are observed is quite another. The ILO examines how governments are putting the standards into practice through legislation and activities. It can shame governments in the eyes of the international community. In the end, though, the ILO can only persuade governments; it cannot force them.

The Fundamental Rights

In 1998, the ILO adopted the Declaration on Fundamental Principles and Rights at Work. This says that certain rights are so fundamental that they apply to all workers, irrespective of whether or not their governments have signed up to the relevant Conventions, and no matter how rich or poor their country is. They are called the 'core labour standards'. They are:

⇨ The right to form trade unions ('freedom of association').

⇨ The right to effective collective bargaining between workers and management.

⇨ Freedom from forced or compulsory labour.

⇨ An end to child labour.

⇨ Freedom from discrimination in the workplace.

All ILO member states are obliged to promote and realise these fundamental rights. It is clear, however, that many governments are ignoring their duties. They are instead undermining workers' fundamental rights in the interests of attracting investors in the global economy.

Core labour standards are basic human rights that help people break out of the poverty trap. They are the building blocks of democracy, and crucial to the empowerment of working people, especially the poor and marginalised.

Respect for the fundamental rights of people at work is essential if there is to be economic, social and political development for the whole world.

No forced labour

No-one should be compelled to work, without exception. This is according to two core labour standards of the ILO which aim to eliminate all forms of forced or compulsory labour.

ILO Convention on Forced Labour, No. 29 (1930) bans all forms of forced or compulsory labour, except for military service or convict labour, or during emergencies such as war, fires and earthquakes.

Forced labour ranges from slavery to trafficking in human beings

ILO Convention on the Abolition of Forced Labour, No. 105 (1957) bans the use of compulsory labour as a means of political coercion or education, to mobilise or discipline a workforce, as a punishment for taking part in a strike, or as a means of discrimination.

Yet still these abhorrent practices continue today. Lack of political will and vested interests in many countries keep millions of people enslaved or entrapped.

'I became bonded after I got married to my husband twenty years ago – his family had been bonded for three generations to the same landlord – they took loans for marriage, for illness, for education... I used to work from 6am in the landlord's house, cleaning, fetching water... Then I would go and work on the farm... cutting, threshing... until 7pm or later. Sometimes I would then go back to the house to clean everything. Only after that could I go home and feed my family. We were not allowed to work for any other landlord.'

Leelu Bai, former bonded labourer, Thane District, India

Forced or compulsory labour ranges from slavery and debt bondage to trafficking in human beings. The United Nations estimates that there are around 12.3 million bonded labourers around the world. On farms in South Asia and Africa, as well as in certain other industries, millions of men, women, and children are tied to their work through a vicious circle of debt.

The cross-border trafficking of women and children is also increasing, involving over 800,000 a year around the world. They are traded for prostitution and domestic service, and for work in sweatshops. In the Republic of Ireland and Northern Ireland, agencies working in the field report increased evidence of women from

Eastern Europe, Africa and elsewhere being trafficked, with Ireland as their destination or *en route* to other European countries.

International action against Burma's military rulers

In November 2000, the ILO took the unprecedented step of calling on all governments to take sanctions against the country of Burma, now also called Myanmar. The ILO charged the Burmese military regime with a 'crime against humanity' for its systematic use of forced labour.

Up to two million men, women, children and the elderly are forced to work for the Burmese military. They construct roads, railways, dams and army camps. They act as servants and sentries for army officers. Or they dig fish-ponds, log timber and farm on land that officers have seized. Porters are saddled with heavy loads and force-marched through the hills, often in front to detonate mines.

Burma has ratified ILO Conventions on freedom of association and freedom from forced labour, but ignores them. The Federation of Trade Unions of Burma (FTUB) is banned and two of its leaders, U Khin Kyaw and U Myo Aung Thant, have been jailed for 17 years and life respectively for their union activities. The FTUB operates in exile from Thailand.

Global Unions has released a database of over 325 foreign companies with business links to Burma. Some prominent companies have withdrawn under international union pressure, such as the French multinational hotel chain Accor. But Global Unions is still adding other firms to the list who are happy to do business with Burma and its vicious junta.

An end to child labour

Child labour is still rife around the world. No country or region is immune. Crises such as natural disasters, economic downturns, the HIV/AIDS pandemic and armed conflicts increasingly draw the young into child labour. Millions are employed on farms or in the so-called 'informal' economy. Others are used as very cheap labour in sweatshops, making consumer goods such as carpets and toys, or in restaurants, and even in mines and quarries.

The ILO estimates that more than 200 million children – one in every six children aged five to 17 – are doing work that is damaging to their mental, physical and emotional development. Children work because their survival and that of their families depend on it. Child labour persists even where it has been declared illegal, and is frequently surrounded by a wall of silence, indifference and apathy. But that wall is beginning to crumble. While the total elimination of child labour is

a long-term goal in many countries, certain forms of child labour must be confronted immediately. The ILO has two core labour standards relating to child labour:

⇨ ILO Convention on the Minimum Age of Entry into Employment, No. 138 (1973) says that governments must have a national policy to ensure the effective abolition of child labour.

⇨ ILO Convention on the Worst Forms of Child Labour, No. 182 (1999) sets out the first steps that governments must take to eliminate the worst forms of child labour.

Ending child labour is not a simple issue. Taking children out of employment may push them onto the streets. Therefore family incomes must rise by paying fair wages. The ILO International Programme for the Elimination of Child Labour (IPEC) is active in over 90 countries, its SCREAM – Supporting Children's Rights through Education, the Arts and the Media – programme is the main tool to promote children's participation and youth empowerment and has been translated into 19 languages.

The ILO estimates that more than 200 million children are doing work that is damaging to their mental, physical and emotional development

On 12 June 2002, the ILO launched the International Day Against Child Labour to keep up the international momentum to stop child labour, especially its worst forms.

In a 2006 report, ILO could confirm: 'We are beginning to see an encouraging reduction in child labour – especially in its worst forms – in many areas of the world. From 2002–2006 child labourers fell by 11 per cent'. The IPEC played an important role in this progress, as well as an important political and NGO mobilisation in many countries around the world. The Irish Congress of Trade Unions has been an active member in the Irish Task Force against Child Labour and in the Global Campaign for Education.

Congress' active work was of utmost importance to realise the third phase of the Irish Aid/International Labour Organization partnership programme. The third phase of the partnership programmes includes a €1 million support from Irish Aid to ILO's special programme to eliminate Child Labour (IPEC). It was launched on 4 November 2008 in the Irish Aid volunteering centre in Dublin. This was also the official opening of the Irish

Aid- and ICTU-sponsored exhibition of photographs on the subject of 'Ethiopian women with disabilities at work'.

Partly as a result of the publicity generated from the Global March Against Child Labour, the Republic of Ireland was the first European Union country to ratify ILO Convention No. 182 to combat the worst forms of child labour.

Yet the Republic itself still has no national programme of action. According to teachers' unions, children's performance in school is affected by the long part-time hours many work during the school term. The Labour Inspectorate takes few offending employers to court. The ICTU wants to see more done to combat child labour in the Republic.

⇨ The above information is reproduced with kind permission from the Irish Congress of Trade Unions. Visit www.ictu.ie for further information.

© 2012 ICTU

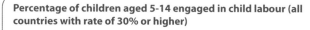

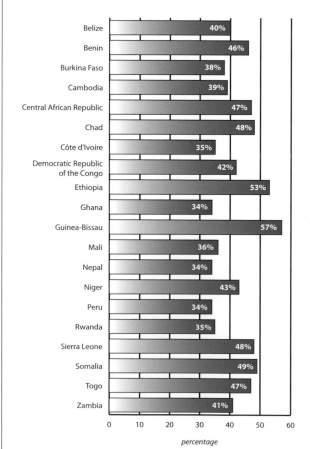

Percentage of children aged 5-14 engaged in child labour (all countries with rate of 30% or higher)

Country	Percentage
Belize	40%
Benin	46%
Burkina Faso	38%
Cambodia	39%
Central African Republic	47%
Chad	48%
Côte d'Ivoire	35%
Democratic Republic of the Congo	42%
Ethiopia	53%
Ghana	34%
Guinea-Bissau	57%
Mali	36%
Nepal	34%
Niger	43%
Peru	34%
Rwanda	35%
Sierra Leone	48%
Somalia	49%
Togo	47%
Zambia	41%

percentage

Definition of child labour:
Age 5/11 years: At least one hour of economic work or 28 hours of domestic work per week.
Age 12/14 years: At least 14 hours of economic work or 28 hours of domestic work per week.

Source: UNICEF Global Databases, Child Protection: Child Labour, *January 2012.* © UNICEF

An overview of human trafficking

Information from the Serious Organised Crime Agency.

The legal definition:

The definition of human trafficking commonly accepted by governments, law enforcement bodies and agencies, including the UK Human Trafficking Centre (UKHTC), derives from the UN Protocol to Prevent, Suppress and Punish Trafficking in Persons, especially women and children, supplementing the UN Convention Against Transnational Organisational Crime. This is also commonly referred to as 'the Palermo Protocol'.

According to Article 3, 'Trafficking in Persons' means:

'The recruitment, transportation, transfer, harbouring or receipt of persons, by means of the threat or use of force or other forms of coercion, of abduction, of fraud, of deception, of the abuse of power, or a position of vulnerability, or the giving or receiving of payments or benefits to achieve the consent of a person having control over another person, for the purpose of exploitation. Exploitation shall include, at a minimum, the exploitation of the prostitution of others or other forms of sexual exploitation, forced labour or services, slavery or practices similar to slavery, servitude or the removal or organs'.

Children cannot give consent to being moved, therefore the coercion or deception elements do not have to be present.

Source, transit and destination countries throughout Europe translate and interpret the Palermo Protocol in different ways, so the definition of what constitutes human trafficking can differ between nations.

A working definition:

In the simplest terms, human trafficking is the movement of a person from one place to another into conditions of exploitation using deception, coercion, the abuse of power or the abuse of someone's vulnerability. It is entirely possible to have been a victim of trafficking even if your consent has been given to being moved.

There are therefore three constituent elements:

⇨ The movement – recruitment, transportation, transfer, harbouring or receipt of persons.

⇨ The control – threat, use of force, coercion, abduction, fraud, deception, abuse of power or vulnerability, or the giving of payments or benefits to a person in control of the victim.

⇨ The purpose – exploitation of a person, which includes prostitution and other sexual exploitation, forced labour, slavery or similar practices, and the removal of organs.

Although human trafficking often involves an international cross-border element, it is also possible to be a victim of human trafficking within your own country.

Types of human trafficking

There are four broad categories of exploitation linked to human trafficking:

Sexual exploitation

Sexual exploitation involves any non-consensual or abusive sexual acts performed without a victim's permission. This includes, but is not limited to, prostitution, escort work and pornography. Women, men and children of both sexes can be victims. Many will have been deceived with promises of a better life and then controlled through violence and abuse.

Forced labour

Forced labour involves victims being compelled to work very long hours, often in arduous conditions, and to hand over the majority, if not all, of their wages to their traffickers. Forced labour crucially implies the use of coercion and lack of freedom or choice for the victim. In many cases victims are subjected to verbal threats or violence to achieve compliance.

Manufacturing, entertainment, travel, farming and construction industries throughout the world have been found to use forced labour by victims of human trafficking to some extent, with a marked increase in reported numbers in recent years. Often large numbers of individuals are housed in single dwellings and there is evidence of 'hot bunking', where a returning shift takes up the sleeping accommodation of those starting the next shift.

The International Labour Organization has identified six elements which individually or collectively can indicate forced labour. These are:

⇨ threats or actual physical harm;

⇨ restriction of movement and confinement to the workplace or to a limited area;

⇨ debt bondage;

⇨ withholding of wages or excessive wage reductions that violate previously-made agreements;

⇨ retention of passports and identity documents (the workers can neither leave nor prove their identity status); and

⇨ threat of denunciation to the authorities where the worker is of illegal status.

SERIOUS ORGANISED CRIME AGENCY

Domestic servitude

Domestic servitude involves the victim being forced to work in private households. Their movement will often be restricted and they will be forced to perform household tasks such as childcare and housekeeping over long hours and for little, if any, pay.

Victims will lead very isolated lives and have little or no unsupervised freedom. Their own privacy and comfort will be minimal, often sleeping on a mattress on the floor in an open part of the house.

In rare circumstances where victims receive a wage it will be heavily reduced, ostensibly to pay for food and accommodation.

Organ harvesting

Organ harvesting involves trafficking people in order to use their internal organs for transplant. The illegal trade is dominated by kidneys, which are in the greatest demand and are the only major organs that can be wholly transplanted with relatively few risks to the life of the donor.

Common myths

Myth: Human trafficking and people smuggling is the same thing

There are important differences between human trafficking and people smuggling.

The principal difference is the element of exploitation.

People being smuggled as illegal migrants have usually consented to being smuggled. Trafficking victims have not consented, or the consent they did give is rendered meaningless by the actions of the traffickers, for example deception.

What happens to each of them at the end of their journey will be very different too. The relationship between an illegal migrant and a people smuggler is a commercial transaction which ends on completion of the journey. However, for those who have been trafficked, the very purpose of the journey is to put them into a situation where they can be exploited on an ongoing basis for the sake of the traffickers' profits. The journey is only the beginning. It can nevertheless be difficult to distinguish between trafficking and smuggling scenarios for many reasons, including:

⇨ People who begin as smuggled migrants may inadvertently become victims of trafficking, i.e. there is a change of circumstances at some point during the process;

⇨ The same people acting as traffickers may also act as smugglers and use the same routes for both trafficking and smuggling;

⇨ Conditions for smuggled persons may be so bad that it is difficult to believe that they consented to it.

Myth: You cannot be a victim of trafficking if you gave your consent to be moved

Someone becomes a victim of trafficking not only because of the journey they are forced to make but because of the exploitation to which they are exposed at the end of that journey, and to which they have not consented.

Any consent they do give to make the journey in the first place is likely to have been gained fraudulently, for example with the promise of a job or a better standard of living.

This is why the Palermo Protocol makes clear that human trafficking is about the three elements of movement, control and exploitation.

Myth: Trafficking only affects people from other countries

Whilst people smuggling always involves illegal border crossing and entry into another country, human trafficking for exploitation can happen within someone's own country, including Britain.

Myth: Many trafficked women are already prostitutes

This is a common misconception. The majority of trafficking victims working as prostitutes will have been forced into it against their will, having already been trafficked without their consent, deceived into consenting to the journey, or deceived about the kind of work they would be doing at the end of the journey.

⇨ The above information is reprinted with kind permission from the Serious Organised Crime Agency (SOCA). Visit www.soca.gov.uk for more information.

© SOCA Serious Organised Crime Agency 2012

SERIOUS ORGANISED CRIME AGENCY

Sex trafficking and prostitution

How does sex trafficking relate to prostitution?

There is a clear link between sex trafficking and prostitution. The demand for paid sexual services creates:

⇨ The need for a supply of trafficked women.

⇨ The opportunity for criminal gangs to make money from trafficking women to meet that need.

We therefore believe that you cannot end sex trafficking without addressing the demand for paid sexual services.

Would legalising prostitution give trafficked women more rights?

No. We believe that the legalisation of prostitution would increase the proliferation of sex trafficking, because it promotes the view of prostitution as a victimless crime and 'normalises' the purchase of sexual favours for money.

So would you criminalise men who buy sex from women?

Yes, we believe new legislation is needed to criminalise men who buy sex from women in the UK. In Britain, it is currently not unlawful to pay for sex and this creates a market for sex trafficking.

Criminalising the purchase of sexual acts, such as has been proven to work in the Nordic European states, will help tackle sex trafficking in a number of ways:

⇨ It gives a clear message that the exploitation of women is unacceptable;

⇨ It destroys the market for sex trafficking;

⇨ It allows the prosecution service to use the testimony of punters to prosecute sex traffickers and so takes the burden of truth away from the sex trafficking survivor;

⇨ It makes those causing harm accountable for their actions;

⇨ It decriminalises those who sell sex acts whilst offering support services to exit prostitution.

Are people aware of the harm they cause by paying for sex?

Many men would not pay for sex if they knew the harm they were creating by fuelling sex trafficking and that their acts are perpetuating rape, violence and slavery. We need to ensure that people are aware of the realities of sex trafficking and its causes and consequences so that we can all make an informed choice.

But prostitution is the oldest profession in the world – you will never end it

Just because something has been around for a long time does not mean it's a good thing. Slavery was a legal trade for many years, but the international community took a stand against it. Sex trafficking is a modern-day form of slavery that must also be stopped.

How will these women earn a living if these men stop paying for sex with them?

Trafficked women don't receive the money that exchanges hands for their sexual services. This money goes directly to their traffickers and exploiters. The women themselves are kept as prisoners, their passports are confiscated and they are forced to sleep with as many as 50 men a day for nothing.

What about women who choose to work in prostitution?

We understand that some women will and do choose to work in prostitution and we respect their right to do this and to organise for better rights.

However, for the vast majority of women working in prostitution, and particularly trafficked women who are coerced or forced, they do not have a choice.

sexual slavery

ANTI-TRAFFICKING ALLIANCE

Sex trafficking and the 2012 London Olympics

Will the London Olympics increase sex trafficking into the UK?

In 2012, the eyes of the world will be on London as it hosts the Olympic and Paralympic Games. Sport can be a positive force in the lives of Londoners, but major sporting events have also been linked with increases in trafficking, prostitution and sexual assault in the past.

We are concerned that traffickers will seek to profit from the 2012 Games and would like the UK Government to do everything it can to prevent this and reduce the risk to vulnerable women.

Past events have shown sex trafficking surge

Evidence from previous sporting events suggests that a surge in the number of visitors to a country can lead to an increased demand for prostitution – and an increase in trafficking to meet this demand:

⇨ The Metropolitan Police has already noted a small increase in the number of trafficked women working in the five Olympic host boroughs of London. (Guardian *article, 19 July 2009*)

⇨ There were reports of sex attacks in the athletes' village at Sydney in 2000. (Guardian *article, 19 July 2009*)

⇨ A report by a leading counter-human trafficking organisation in Canada outlines a link between international sporting events and an upsurge in the demand for prostitution from visitors, site workers and athletes which in turn fuels human trafficking. (*The Future Group, 2007*)

⇨ At the Athens Olympic Games in 2004, where prevention efforts were poor, the number of known human trafficking victims almost doubled. (*The Future Group, 2007*)

⇨ The European Parliament recognised in their resolution passed on 15 March 2006 that major sporting events result in a 'temporary and spectacular increase in the demand for sexual services'.

⇨ Organisations working to protect children have highlighted how the largest sporting event in the US, the Superbowl, coincides with a spike in trafficking of underage girls – at previous Superbowls pimps have hired cab drivers to turn their vehicles into mobile brothels, according to one activist. (The Independent, *6 February 2011*)

Is there really a surge in sex trafficking?

Not everyone agrees with these findings – a researcher at George Washington University, for example, states that claims of increases are overblown or inaccurate. (Weitzer, R, 2007)

Part of the problem is that the nature of sex trafficking makes it very difficult to assess any increase and to collect accurate data.

A report into sex trafficking and the German World Cup (International Organization for Migration, 2006), for example, found that media reports that 40,000 women might be trafficked into Germany were unfounded and unrealistic.

However, the report also found that prevention campaigns and increased law enforcement efforts may have reduced the risk of trafficking and the characteristics of the fan base – mostly families with children – was also likely to reduce the demand for sexual services.

Whether there is an increase in trafficking or not in 2012, the Olympic Games are likely to impact on the women already in prostitution in the five Olympic host boroughs. Coordinated and victim-centred policing across the boroughs is essential to ensure that women are not displaced from one borough to another.

What can the UK Government do?

The Anti-Trafficking Alliance has been working in partnership with other anti-trafficking charities, the Equality and Human Rights Commission, the Metropolitan Police Service and the Greater London Authority to develop prevention plans and activities prior to the 2012 Games.

We want to see:

1 A major public awareness-raising campaign about the causes and consequences of sex trafficking – and its links to prostitution – with the result that visitors to London are aware of the UK legislation on paying for sex with coerced individuals and the sexual exploitation of children under 18.

2 Training for health workers and other frontline service-providers to ensure:

⇨ Specialist trafficking teams are set up at UK ports and airports.

⇨ An advice line and training for police, immigration staff, social workers, health workers and other frontline staff are in place so they can support and respond to the needs of victims of trafficking.

⇨ The removal of advertising for sex services in newspapers.

⇨ Effective enforcement action against those who pay for sex with someone subject to force and against traffickers.

⇨ Information from the Anti-Trafficking Alliance. Visit www.atalliance.org.uk for further information.

© 2012 Anti-Trafficking Alliance

UK complicity in torture

Information from Liberty.

Human rights law bans the use of torture or inhuman or degrading treatment or punishment. This requires not only that countries do not engage in torture or subject people to ill treatment, but that they don't condone or become complicit in torture or ill treatment. Yet over the past few years, increasing evidence has come to light of UK knowledge of, and involvement in, the CIA's post-9/11 programme of extraordinary rendition and torture and in attempts to use information obtained through the use of torture as evidence in UK courts.

Torture evidence

One aspect of UK complicity in torture is past attempts to use information gained by torture in legal cases. This contravenes the United Nations Convention Against Torture, which explicitly forbids the use of such 'evidence' in legal proceedings. In December 2005, in a case Liberty intervened in, the House of Lords confirmed that the use of evidence derived from torture was unlawful, regardless of who carried out the torture. It held that the ban on torture and other forms of ill treatment is absolute and cannot be opted out of. The use of 'evidence' that might have been obtained in violation of that ban is therefore unlawful.

UK assistance in or encouragement of torture

In recent years a number of people who have been subjected to torture and other ill treatment in

Guantánamo Bay, Afghanistan, Pakistan, Egypt, Morocco and elsewhere have alleged that UK officials knew of their ill treatment and not only did nothing to prevent it, but actively assisted their abusers.

The High Court has found in relation to Mr Binyam Mohamed, a former Guantánamo Bay detainee, that UK security services helped US authorities interrogate Mr Mohamed, although they knew that he was being detained incommunicado and in cruel, inhuman and degrading conditions. There is also evidence that UK officials may have passed on information to their American counterparts which was then used in abducting and subjecting people to extraordinary rendition and in interrogations.

In July 2010, the Government announced an inquiry into the mistreatment of detainees abroad and the extent of UK knowledge. Liberty is pushing to ensure that this inquiry has a broad remit and is granted powers to compel witnesses and take evidence.

Closed hearings and secret evidence

In recent times, extraordinary steps have been taken to keep any information about possible UK complicity in torture secret. The previous Government sought to use principles of public interest immunity to restrict access to government documents and to suppress parts of a court judgment in the case of Binyam Mohamed which outlined what the UK knew about torture and ill treatment of detainees in US custody. It has also unsuccessfully attempted to have a 'closed-material' procedure before the High Court in a civil claim against the UK Government for involvement in ill treatment and unlawful detention by US authorities.

⇨ Information from Liberty. Visit www.liberty-human-rights.org.uk for more.

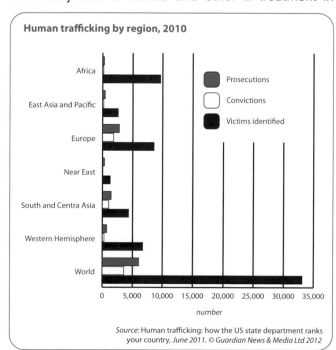

Human trafficking by region, 2010

Legend: Prosecutions, Convictions, Victims identified

Regions (top to bottom): Africa, East Asia and Pacific, Europe, Near East, South and Centra Asia, Western Hemisphere, World

x-axis: 0, 5,000, 10,000, 15,000, 20,000, 25,000, 30,000, 35,000

number

Source: Human trafficking: how the US state department ranks your country, *June 2011. © Guardian News & Media Ltd 2012*

LIBERTY

Obtained under torture

Information from YouGov.

By Hannah Thompson and Krista Campbell

Almost half of British adults believe that in some circumstances, British security services could be justified in using information obtained under torture elsewhere, compared to just over a third that this would never be acceptable, our survey on the subject has discovered, as allegations of Libyan rendition by MI6 continue to surface. Prime Minister David Cameron and French President Nicolas Sarkozy were welcomed yesterday in Libyan rebel stronghold Benghazi, as they sought to re-establish diplomatic relations with the nation state.

⇨ 46% of British people thought that there were some instances in which British security services could be justified in using information from other countries which has been obtained through the use of torture.

⇨ 34% decided that there were no circumstances in which this would be acceptable.

⇨ 19% said they were unsure.

> **Almost half of British adults believe that in some circumstances, British security services could be justified in using information obtained under torture elsewhere**

Allegations of rendition

The results come amid recent allegations in light of the ongoing situation in Libya, in which it has emerged that the British Secret Intelligence Service (MI6) may have been closely involved in the rendition of Libyan terror suspects, while the discovery of some papers in Tripoli suggest close ties between MI6, the CIA and the Gaddafi regime.

The Gibson Inquiry, set up last year by David Cameron, is said to be considering new allegations of UK involvement in rendition to Libya.

Cameron has said that he wants to 'deal with these accusations of malpractice so as to enable our security services to get on with the vital work that they do', in the same week as he and French President Nicolas Sarkozy visit rebel-held city Benghazi to re-establish diplomatic relations with the country.

Then-terrorist suspect Abdel Hakim Belhaj, commander of anti-government forces in Tripoli, is certain that he was involved in an MI6 rendition operation in 2004. He said, 'What happened to me and my family is illegal. It deserves an apology. And for what happened to me when I was captured and tortured.'

> **Cameron has said that he wants to 'deal with these accusations of malpractice so as to enable our security services to get on with the vital work that they do'**

Co-operation: The right thing to do?

The allegations of co-operation between the countries have not been entirely dismissed by some, who suggest that some British co-operation with Libya was necessary to diffuse then-leader Gaddafi's plan to develop mass destruction weapons. As our recent polling shows, many British people feel that co-operating with the dictator was 'the right thing to do' – although our previous questions did not deal explicitly with torture.

Former head of the MI5 security service Eliza Manningham-Buller, however, is unequivocal. She told the BBC: 'torture is wrong and never justified'.

19 September 2011

⇨ The above information is reproduced with kind permission from YouGov. Visit www.yougov.com for further information.

© YouGov plc

UK torture complicity inquiry 'scrapped'

The long-awaited inquiry into British complicity in torture is to be scrapped following the launch of fresh criminal investigations into claims of ill treatment in Libya, the Justice Secretary has said.

Ken Clarke told MPs on Wednesday afternoon there 'now appears no prospect of the Gibson Inquiry being able to start in the foreseeable future'.

However, he said the Government still intends to hold 'an independent, judge-led inquiry once all police investigations have concluded'.

Clarke said: 'We remain committed to drawing a line under these issues.

'However, these further investigations may take some considerable time to conclude. The Government fully intends to hold a judge-led inquiry into these issues once it is possible to do so and all related police investigations have been concluded.

The detainee inquiry had already been widely criticised for lacking 'credibility or transparency', with human rights groups and lawyers for detainees refusing to take part

'But there now appears no prospect of the Gibson Inquiry being able to start in the foreseeable future.

'So, following consultation with Sir Peter Gibson, the inquiry chair, we have decided to bring the work of this inquiry to a conclusion.'

He went on: 'We will continue to keep Parliament fully informed of progress.

'The Government fully intends to hold an independent, judge-led inquiry, once all police investigations have concluded, to establish the full facts and draw a line under these issues.'

Clarke said it would have been unfair to the inquiry team to continue keeping it on hold for an 'as yet unknown period of time' while the Libyan investigations were carried out.

Scotland Yard took three years looking into the cases of Guantánamo Bay detainees, he said.

The detainee inquiry had already been widely criticised for lacking 'credibility or transparency', with human

rights groups and lawyers for detainees refusing to take part.

Campaigners, who are angry at the limits on the inquiry's powers and the fact that the final decision on whether material can be made public rested with the Government, also claimed the police investigation was being 'hobbled' by political pressure for a 'sham' inquiry.

Shami Chakrabarti, director of the civil rights group Liberty, said: 'We welcome the sensible decision to end the embarrassment of a so-called inquiry in which neither torture victims nor human rights campaigners had faith'

Shami Chakrabarti, director of the civil rights group Liberty, said: 'We welcome the sensible decision to end the embarrassment of a so-called inquiry in which neither torture victims nor human rights campaigners had faith.

'Let's remember that it was lawyers, journalists and campaigners that uncovered the Libyan rendition files now to be properly investigated by police and prosecutors.

'Such revelations should lead to more scrutiny of the secret state, not the shutting down of open justice as proposed in the Government's current Green Paper.'

It comes after police and prosecutors said last week that allegations from two Libyan rebels, Sami al Saadi and Abdel Hakim Belhadj, that British spies were complicit in their rendition and ill treatment in 2004 were so serious that they must be investigated immediately.

18 January 2012

⇨ The above information is reprinted with kind permission from the Press Association. Visit www.pressassociation.com for more information on this and other related topics.

© 2012 Press Association

PRESS ASSOCIATION

Issues surrounding children's rights

Information from UNICEF.

About your rights

Every child and young person under the age of 18 has rights, no matter who they are, where they live or what they believe in. These rights are protected by an agreement between almost all of the countries in the world.

On 20 November 1989, the world made a set of promises to all children when it adopted the United Nations Convention on the Rights of the Child. All of the countries in the world have now signed up to it except for Somalia and the United States of America. A convention is an agreement between countries to obey the same law.

The Convention states that every child has the same rights:

⇨ the right to a childhood (which includes protection from harm);

⇨ the right to be educated (which includes all girls and boys completing primary school);

⇨ the right to be healthy (which includes having clean water, nutritious food and medical care);

⇨ the right to be treated fairly (which includes changing laws and practices that are unfair on children);

⇨ the right to be heard (which includes considering children's views).

The Convention is needed because people under the age of 18 need unique care and protection that adults don't. It says that children are entitled to these rights whatever their race, religion, abilities, or type of family they come from. With these rights come responsibilities. Every child, young person and adult has a responsibility to make sure that their behaviour doesn't interfere with another person's rights.

Governments are responsible for making these rights available to everyone, and making sure that all parents and children know and understand the Convention. All organisations concerned with children should work towards what is best for them.

Rights in the UK

The United Kingdom ratified the UN Convention on the Rights of the Child on 16 December 1991. That means that our Government now has to make sure that every child has all the rights in the Convention. They have to regularly report to a panel of independent experts, and deliver progress updates explaining the efforts they've made towards child rights.

Health

Every child has the right to healthcare, clean water, nutritious food and a safe environment so they can be as healthy as possible.

Yet in 2008, nearly nine million children died before their fifth birthday, and most of these deaths could have been prevented. Around 4,000 children die every day from diarrhoea because they don't have access to clean drinking water or proper sanitation, like toilets. Others die because they do not have enough food to eat.

Vaccines are injections that help prevent children from catching diseases like tuberculosis. UNICEF delivers more vaccines to developing countries than any other organisation. In 2008, we delivered vaccines to 56 per cent of the world's children, as well as 19 million mosquito nets, which keep mosquitos away from children at night and prevent the spread of malaria.

We also run programmes around the world to prevent mothers from passing on HIV to their babies (prevention of mother-to-child transmission), and we work to make sure children have clean water and proper toilet facilities.

In emergencies, UNICEF provides clean water and sanitation facilities like toilets to children whose homes have been washed away by floods or destroyed by an earthquake. In places where there is a lack of food, we train health workers like doctors and nurses, and deliver things like therapeutic food (ready-to-eat food which is very nutritious and high in energy) to treat children with malnutrition.

Working with local governments, UNICEF helps to build health systems like hospitals and doctors' surgeries, or to re-build them after an emergency, leading to long-lasting benefits for children. We go deep and tackle the very causes.

Education

Every child has the right to an education, which develops their personality, talents and abilities to the full. Primary education must be free for all children.

UNICEF

But around the world, more than 100 million children, the majority of them girls, are still denied their right to go to school. Poor teaching, school buildings and equipment, or poverty, mean that many others don't get the chance to fulfil their potential.

Primary school education is not free in many countries, and the cost means many families aren't able to send their children to school. UNICEF is helping governments abolish school fees in countries such as Mozambique, Uganda, Togo and Kenya. In Kenya, UNICEF has provided £1.5 million to buy education materials like books and pencils, to train teachers and to repair school buildings.

Many children, especially girls, miss out on an education because it is seen as their job to help out with household chores, such as fetching water for the family. UNICEF works with communities and governments to change attitudes and make sure girls are treated fairly.

For too many children who do go to school, it is not as good an experience as it should be. UNICEF works to make sure that the education children receive is of good quality through our Child-Friendly School (CFS) model. These schools are protective environments with trained teachers and good equipment. We also work to make sure that schools have safe water and proper sanitation, including separate toilets for boys and girls.

In the UK, UNICEF works to make sure everyone in school respects each others' rights through UNICEF UK's Rights Respecting Schools Award (RRSA).

Childhood

The UN Convention on the Rights of the Child recognises that childhood is a crucial time for a child to grow and develop, and also a time where people are most vulnerable, meaning they need extra protection compared to adults.

By adopting the Convention, the world has promised every child extra care, protection and chances to rest and play, which they need to make sure they are not abused or forced to take on adult responsibilities.

Although progress has been made, many children are still denied their right to a childhood. Millions are homeless and living on city streets around the world. Around one child in six worldwide is forced to work to earn money, sometimes in dangerous conditions.

Other children are bought and sold, neglected or hurt. About 1.2 million children worldwide have been trafficked – taken away from their home, often to another country – and forced to work for little money or are sold for sex. Some children have to grow up too quickly because they have to care for sick parents or for their brothers and sisters, with no one to care for them in turn.

UNICEF works with governments and within the UN to put laws in place which protect children against exploitation, including child labour and trafficking.

We work with families to tackle the reasons why children are forced into the workplace and we give training and support to children who have been living on the streets or working.

We support communities to give care and protection to orphaned and vulnerable children and we work with partners to make sure that children can play and practise sport.

Voice

Every child has the right to a voice and a say in matters that affect them. They must also have their views taken seriously according to their age and maturity.

UNICEF works with children, not just for them, both in our own work and by encouraging the involvement of children and young people in decisions that affect them. Children will have to deal with the consequences of the decisions adults make today on issues such as HIV and AIDS, climate change and poverty, so it is important that their views be considered by decision-makers.

We created the Junior 8 summit (J8), a young person's version of the annual G8 summit. The J8 gives young people from both G8 and non-G8 countries the opportunity to come together to discuss how they could change the world for the better.

UNICEF

Ahead of the Copenhagen Climate Conference summit in 2009, UNICEF and the City of Copenhagen hosted the Children's Climate Forum, giving young people a voice in the global climate change debate and an opportunity to influence decision-makers.

UNICEF recognises that if we listen to young people we can create better, more relevant and more long-lasting programmes and policies, meaning we can better protect all their other rights. In 15 countries around the world, for instance, UNICEF has involved young people as researchers, programme designers and communicators in the Right to Know initiative to help young people make informed decisions about how to prevent HIV infections.

We reach out to the children whose voices are most likely to go unheard and provide opportunities for them to express their views freely. We support programmes such as photo workshops and child-to-child radio programmes so children and young people can express themselves on issues that affect them.

Fairness

All children have the same rights, no matter where they're from, whether they're a boy or a girl, what religion they belong to or whether they are HIV-positive or not. They have the same rights no matter what their family background is or whether they are disabled or not. Yet every day children, like adults, are discriminated against for any number of reasons. Poverty is also a huge barrier that denies children their rights.

Children have the same rights even if they do not have the nationality of the country they are living in. In 2008, after UNICEF UK put pressure on the UK Government, the Government removed its last two reservations to the UN Convention on the Child, including one on immigration and nationality. This means that children who have fled their country and come to the UK seeking asylum, and children who have been trafficked into the UK and exploited, often forced to work, now have the same rights, such as to education and health, as British children.

Through our community-based programmes, UNICEF works to end cultural traditions and practices that harm children, and violence against children because of their gender.

Children and young people affected by HIV are often denied their rights because of discrimination or because they or their parents don't have access to the right treatment. UNICEF supports children affected by HIV with funding and services including healthcare and counselling.

Here in the UK, the fifth richest country in the world, around four million children live in poverty. UNICEF UK, as a member of the End Child Poverty coalition, is working to make sure that the UK Government keeps its promise to end child poverty in the UK by 2020.

Children have the same rights even if they do not have the nationality of the country they are living in

⇨ The above information is reprinted with kind permission from UNICEF. Visit their website www.tagd.org.uk for more.

© UNICEF UK

Fast facts

Here are some handy facts about the CRC which you could use to organise a quiz night in your area and fundraise for your chosen cause.

⇨ There are 54 articles in the Convention.

⇨ The UK Government signed the CRC in 1990 and made a commitment to realise children's rights in the UK.

⇨ Each government that has signed up to the CRC must report to the UN Committee on the Rights of the Child in Geneva every five years to state its progress in making the Convention a reality in that country.

⇨ The Committee is a UN treaty monitoring body. It examines each country's report and also looks at evidence from other bodies such as the Children's Commissioner's office. The Committee then makes recommendations to the Government for ways it can move forward to improve child rights in its country.

⇨ Last year the Committee made over 100 observations and recommendations to the UK Government and, whilst it praised the progress that had been made, it pointed out that there is still much to be done, particularly on issues such as child poverty.

⇨ Article 12 states that children and young people should be listened to and their views taken into account. UNICEF UK runs the Rights Respecting School Award which puts the CRC at the heart of a school.

⇨ The Convention on the Rights of the Child is currently the most widely ratified international human rights treaty – all UN member states except for the United States and Somalia have ratified (signed up to) the Convention.

⇨ Articles 43 to 54 are about how adults and governments should work together to make sure all children get all their rights.

UNICEF

Millennium Development Goal 2: achieving universal primary education

In September 2000, world leaders came together at United Nations Headquarters to adopt the United Nations Millennium Declaration, committing to a new global partnership to reduce extreme poverty and setting out a series of time-bound targets – with a deadline of 2015 – that have become known as the Millennium Development Goals.

Millennium Development Goal 2: achieve universal primary education

Target

Ensure that by 2015, children everywhere, boys and girls alike, will be able to complete a full course of primary schooling.

Quick facts

⇨ Enrolment in primary education in developing regions reached 89 per cent in 2008, up from 83 per cent in 2000.

⇨ The current pace of progress is insufficient to meet the target by 2015.

⇨ About 69 million school-age children are not in school. Almost half of them (31 million) are in sub-Saharan Africa, and more than a quarter (18 million) are in Southern Asia.

Where do we stand?

Despite great strides in many countries, the target is unlikely to be met. Enrolment in primary education has continued to rise, reaching 89 per cent in the developing world in 2008. Between 1999 and 2008, enrolment increased by 18 percentage points in sub-Saharan Africa, and by 11 and eight percentage points in Southern Asia and Northern Africa, respectively.

But the pace of progress is insufficient to ensure that, by 2015, all girls and boys complete a full course of primary schooling. To achieve the goal by the target date, all children at official entry age for primary schooling would have had to be attending classes by 2009. Instead, in half of the sub-Saharan African countries with available data, at least one in four children of enrolment age was not attending school in 2008.

About 69 million school-age children were not going to school in 2008, down from 106 million children in 1999. Almost three-quarters of children out of school are in sub-Saharan Africa (31 million) or Southern Asia (18 million). Drop-out rates in sub-Saharan Africa remain high.

Achieving universal primary education requires more than full enrolment. It also means ensuring that children continue to attend classes. In sub-Saharan Africa, more than 30 per cent of primary school students drop out before reaching a final grade.

Moreover, providing enough teachers and classrooms is vital in order to meet demand, most notably in sub-Saharan Africa. It is estimated that double the current number of teachers would be needed in sub-Saharan Africa in order to meet the primary education target by 2015.

What has worked?

Abolishing school fees in Burundi, Ethiopia, Ghana, Kenya, Mozambique, Malawi, Nepal and Tanzania

The abolition of school fees at primary school level has led to a surge in enrolment in a number of countries. In Tanzania, the enrolment ratio had doubled to 99.6 per cent by 2008 compared to 1999 rates. In Ethiopia, net enrolment was 79 per cent in 2008, an increase of 95 per cent since 2000. But the surge in enrolment in developing regions has brought a new set of challenges in providing enough teachers and classrooms.

Investing in teaching infrastructure and resources in Ghana, Nepal and Tanzania

Ghana has recruited retirees and volunteers to meet teacher demand. Additional funds have also been allocated for the provision of temporary classrooms and teaching materials. In Nepal, investment has ensured that more than 90 per cent of students live within 30 minutes of their local school. Also, Tanzania has embarked on an ambitious programme of education reform, building 54,000 classrooms between 2002 and 2006, as well as hiring 18,000 additional teachers.

Promoting education for girls in Botswana, Egypt and Malawi

Egypt's Girls' Education Initiative and Food-for-Education (FFE) programme encourage girls to attend school by providing free education and by constructing and promoting 'girl-friendly schools'. By 2008, more

UN DEPARTMENT OF PUBLIC INFORMATION

than 1,000 schools were built and almost 28,000 students enrolled. In conjunction, the FFE programme provides school meals to 84,000 children in poor and vulnerable communities. Botswana has reduced female drop-out rates by half by implementing re-admission policies. Malawi has been promoting girls' education in grades 1–4 by providing learning materials.

Expanding access to remote and rural areas in Bolivia and Mongolia

Mongolia has introduced mobile schools ('tent schools') to reach children who would otherwise not have regular access to primary education. 100 mobile schools have been providing educational services across 21 provinces. In Bolivia, a bilingual education programme has been introduced for three of the most widely-used indigenous languages. It covered 11 per cent of primary schools in 2002, expanding access to education for indigenous children in remote areas.

What is the UN doing?

⇨ The UN Educational, Scientific and Cultural Organization (UNESCO) supports countries in building quality primary education systems that reach all children, for instance through the Basic Education in Africa Programme, advocating for countries to adopt legal frameworks guaranteeing eight to ten years of uninterrupted basic education.

⇨ In Ethiopia, the UN Population Fund (UNFPA) supports a programme called 'Berhane Hewan', which advocates putting an end to child marriages and keeping girls in school. To encourage families to let the girls complete schooling, girls receive a female sheep upon completing the programme. In Malawi, UNFPA is working with Youth Councils to repeal a law allowing girls as young as 16 to be married and to support campaigns to keep girls in school.

⇨ The World Food Programme (WFP) provides school meals, which act as a strong incentive for parents to send their children to school and help to build the nutritional foundation that is essential for a child's future intellectual development and physical wellbeing. The programme also encourages parents to send more girls to attend classes.

⇨ The UN Economic and Social Commission for Western Asia (ESCWA) partnered with UNESCO to address problems affecting education in politically unstable environments. ESCWA was responsible for infrastructure, while UNESCO took care of training and e-learning. The initiative facilitated capacity-building sessions on education strategy, instructor training and the creation of courses for teaching Arabic to non-Arabic-speaking Iraqi schoolchildren.

Sources

⇨ The Millennium Development Goals Report 2010, United Nations.

⇨ UN MDG Database (mdgs.un.org).

⇨ MDG Monitor Website (www.mdgmonitor.org).

⇨ What Will It Take to Achieve the Millennium Development Goals? – An International Assessment 2010, UN Development Programme (UNDP).

⇨ UN Girls' Education Initiative, UNICEF (www.ungei.org).

⇨ UN Population Fund (UNFPA).

⇨ UN Educational, Scientific and Cultural Organization (UNESCO).

⇨ World Food Programme (WFP).

⇨ UN Regional Commissions, New York Office.

September 2010

⇨ The above information is reproduced with kind permission from the UN Department of Public Information. Visit the UN Millennium Development Goals website at www.un.org/millenniumgoals for more information on this and other related topics.

It was a quiet month at the school. I heard we only got three death threats this time.

UN DEPARTMENT OF PUBLIC INFORMATION

UK 'lagging behind' on children's rights

Baroness Massey argues that the UN Convention on the Rights of the Child should become part of domestic UK legislation.

It is 20 years since the UK Government ratified the UN Convention on the Rights of the Child – has there been significant progress in ensuring children's rights are considered at all levels of decision-making?

'Not at all levels of decision-making.

'I believe there has been quite a bit of lip service, and there's certainly been reference through amendments to bills, by people who are quite keen on the Convention on the Rights of the Child, but I have to say that it's been mainly coming up in amendments from people who have been working, say, for quite a while; people connected with children.

'People get scared when they hear the word "rights" because I think they think that that would be a free-for-all for children to behave irresponsibly'

'I'm speaking about the Lords now, of course, because I don't know about the Commons, but I suspect it might be the same over there as well. It's the keen people who are pushing it all the time and sometimes not getting the responses that we would have hoped for. It has benefited the voluntary sector in their being able to quote it, but I think as far as Parliament is concerned, it has really been a bit of an uphill struggle.'

Why is it so important for the convention to become part of domestic law?

'It would make life easier for all bills really, coming through Parliament, because we could then refer back to the Convention instead of having to go through all of the intricacies of all the different aspects of it when we come to a bill. So I think being able to refer directly back would actually be a lot easier.'

Is the UK Government lagging behind other countries on making children's rights part of domestic legislation?

'Yes, I think it is. As far as I know, and I only know from speaking to various commissioners in other countries, it took us quite a while to get a Children's Commission in England, didn't it? We do seem to be having to push quite strongly on all aspects of the Convention when it comes to bills.'

Why do you think the devolved administrations in Scotland and Wales have been more proactive than the government at Westminster on this issue?

'Possibly because they're smaller. They had Children's Commissions before England, of course. I also think that there have been some quite clear-cut issues, particularly in Wales, which precipitated the appointment of the Judge Commissioner.

'The child molestation stuff in South Wales; I know we've had the same in England, but I think that came before us. I also think that there are people in Scotland and Wales who, for a long time, have been very active in the area of children's rights. Because we are so much more of a complicated structure, it just takes a long time to get through.'

EPOLITIX

In a democratic society, do you not think it is sufficient for the Government to be morally accountable to children?

'I certainly do. I think that one of the problems is that people get scared when they hear the word "rights", because I think they think that that would be a free-for-all for children to behave irresponsibly, when in fact the UNICEF UK's Rights Respecting Schools Award scheme has been brilliant on this, and makes it clear that this is about rights and democracy within the school, and I think that's how we should approach it. But I do think that people get very twitchy about the word "rights".'

Do you think further rights-based legislation might provoke objections by some members of both Houses who are already critical of the Human Rights Act?

'I think it would, but I think that that doesn't stop us from keeping on trying to explain what we mean by the word "rights", it's not a free-for-all. We have to keep going, but I think that the word "rights" is a bit problematic sometimes.'

The UK's children's commissioners are warning that child poverty could rise as the UK tackles its economic problems; do you think any rise in child poverty is directly in conflict with the UN Convention?

'Yes I do, because I think that if you do have child poverty and a rise in child poverty, it does actually affect children's lives in a very significant way in relation to health and wellbeing, in relation to education and in relation to what rights they have. So I think that because poverty has such a dramatic impact on what I would consider to be children's rights, yes it would have an impact on them.'

The Coalition Government last year gave a commitment to give due regard to the Convention on the Rights of the Child. Do you think this has been borne out in their actions?

'No, I think that again it's two things – I think it's partly that people actually don't understand the concept of what Rights of the Child is, and they feel therefore quite scared of it. And I think that children get "tagged on" sometimes as a last-minute thought. For example, the Health Bill, there's been really very little mention of children in that bill as a specific group. And I think that children need to be there as a specific group – so very often, they are not.'

Do you think there is a lack of enthusiasm for children's rights among decision-makers and influencers, particularly at Westminster?

'It depends who you mean as "decision-makers". At the local level it varies a lot. I think that some people at a local government level are very keen on the Rights of the Child, and some aren't. And that varies from place to place. I think that in Westminster there is a lack of understanding, and the lack of knowledge about the UN Convention on the Rights of the Child; if you asked 25 MPs how many of them knew about it, I would guess that half of them would say they hadn't, and certainly more than half would not know any detail about it, and some would again be worried about the issue of rights. I think that there's a lot of work to do on getting the message across about what the Convention on the Rights of the Child means, and what it is, and how it's good for children, and adults, and society in general.'

7 December 2011

⇨ The above information is reprinted with kind permission from Dods Parliamentary Communications Ltd. Visit their website at www.epolitix.com for further information.

© 2012 Dods Parliamentary Communications Ltd

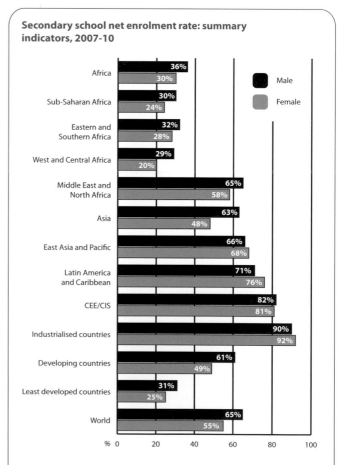

Secondary school net enrolment rate: summary indicators, 2007-10

	Male	Female
Africa	36%	30%
Sub-Saharan Africa	30%	24%
Eastern and Southern Africa	32%	28%
West and Central Africa	29%	20%
Middle East and North Africa	65%	58%
Asia	63%	48%
East Asia and Pacific	66%	68%
Latin America and Caribbean	71%	76%
CEE/CIS	82%	81%
Industrialised countries	90%	92%
Developing countries	61%	49%
Least developed countries	31%	25%
World	65%	55%

Secondary school net enrolment ratio – number of children enrolled in secondary school who are of official secondary school age, expressed as a percentage of the total number of children of official secondary school age. Secondary net enrolment ratio does not include secondary school-aged children enrolled in tertiary education owing to challenges in age reporting and recording at that level.

Source: Secondary School Enrolment and Attendance Rates, January 2012. © UNICEF

UN issues first report on human rights of gay and lesbian people

Information from UN News Centre.

The first ever United Nations report on the human rights of lesbian, gay, bisexual and transgender (LGBT) people details how around the world people are killed or endure hate-motivated violence, torture, detention, criminalisation and discrimination in jobs, healthcare and education because of their real or perceived sexual orientation or gender identity.

The report, released today by the UN Office for the High Commissioner for Human Rights (OHCHR) in Geneva, outlines 'a pattern of human rights violations… that demands a response', and says governments have too often overlooked violence and discrimination based on sexual orientation and gender identity.

Homophobic and transphobic violence has been recorded in every region of the world, the report finds, and ranges from murder, kidnappings, assaults and rapes to psychological threats and arbitrary deprivations of liberty.

LGBT people are often targets of organised abuse from religious extremists, paramilitary groups, neo-Nazis, extreme nationalists and others, as well as family and community violence, with lesbians and transgender women at particular risk.

> **Homophobic and transphobic violence has been recorded in every region of the world … and ranges from murder, kidnappings, assaults and rapes to psychological threats and arbitrary deprivations of liberty**

'Violence against LGBT persons tends to be especially vicious compared to other bias-motivated crimes,' the report notes, citing data indicating that homophobic hate crimes often include 'a high degree of cruelty and brutality.'

Violent incidents or acts of discrimination frequently go unreported because victims do not trust police, are afraid of reprisals or are unwilling to identify themselves as LGBT.

The report – prepared in response to a request from the UN Human Rights Council earlier this year – draws from information included in past UN reporting, official statistics on hate crimes where they are available, and reporting by regional organisations and some non-governmental organisations (NGOs).

In the report, Navi Pillay, the UN High Commissioner for Human Rights, calls on countries to repeal laws that criminalise homosexuality, abolish the death penalty for offences involving consensual sexual relations, harmonise the age of consent for heterosexual and homosexual conduct, and enact comprehensive anti-discrimination laws.

In 76 countries it remains illegal to engage in same-sex conduct and in at least five countries – Iran, Mauritania, Saudi Arabia, Sudan and Yemen – the death penalty prevails.

Ms Pillay recommends that Member States also promptly investigate all killings or serious violent incidents perpetrated because of actual or perceived sexual orientation or gender identity, and to establish systems to record such incidents.

The High Commissioner also calls on countries to ensure that no one fleeing persecution because of their sexual orientation or gender identity is returned to a territory where their life or freedom is at threat, and that asylum laws recognise that sexual orientation or gender identity is a valid basis for claiming persecution.

Public information campaigns should be introduced, especially in schools, to counter homophobia, and police and law enforcement officials should also receive training to ensure LGBT people are treated appropriately and fairly.

Charles Radcliffe, the chief of OHCHR's global issues section, told UN Radio that 'one of the things we found is if the law essentially reflects homophobic sentiment, then it legitimises homophobia in society at large. If the State treats people as second class or second rate or, worse, as criminals, then it's inviting people to do the same thing.'

He stressed that all UN Member States have an obligation under international human rights law to decriminalise homosexuality, adding it was important to persuade rather than lecture States to change their laws.

'I think we have seen the balance of opinion amongst States really shifting significantly in recent years. Some 30 countries have decriminalised homosexuality in the last two decades or so.'

Mr Radcliffe said that while all people have freedom of religion, 'no religious belief or prevailing cultural values can justify stripping people of their basic rights.'

In 76 countries it remains illegal to engage in same-sex conduct

The report, which will be discussed by Council members at a meeting in March next year, has been released as top UN officials have increasingly raised concerns about human rights violations against LGBT people.

Last year, in a speech marking Human Rights Day, Secretary-General Ban Ki-moon said that 'as men and women of conscience, we reject discrimination in general, and in particular discrimination based on sexual orientation or gender identity.'

Ms. Pillay, during a public conversation last week on social media, also called for an end to bullying and other forms of persecution of LGBT people.

15 December 2011

⇨ The above information is reprinted with kind permission from the UN News Centre. Visit www.un.org/news for further information on this and other related topics.

© *UN News Centre*

Government rejects welfare amendments and ignores consequences of DLA cuts

Information from Disability Rights UK.

Disability Rights UK is a membership organisation representing over 500 organisations across the country. We supported the amendments made to the Welfare Reform Bill in the House of Lords, overturned by the Government in the Commons today.

Neil Coyle, Disability Rights UK Director of Policy and Campaigns, says:

'The Government's removal of protections for some disabled people from the Welfare Reform Bill ignores the hundreds of thousands of disabled people directly affected, the hundreds of charities who have highlighted the potential devastating impact for disabled people and their families, the House of Lords who proposed additional protections and the Joint Committee on Human Rights who suggested the Bill will cause destitution.'

Disabled people are disproportionately represented amongst benefit claimants due to lower educational attainment, higher poverty and a lack of accessible work (including through employer discrimination). The Bill aims to cut 280,000 disabled people from receiving out of work benefits altogether and 500,000 disabled people to be made ineligible for a benefit designed to help with disabled people's higher costs of living.

These plans have long-term cost implications being ignored by DWP – including a substantial potential increase in (avoidable) NHS use and rise in demand for council social care services (which many disabled people are being made ineligible for due to council budget cuts).

The Lords had secured protection for some disabled children, disabled adults needing longer than a year to find work and disabled students, for example. Disabled people believed their fears and concerns had been acknowledged and addressed in the House of Lords but this hope has today been removed in the demand for short-term welfare expenditure cuts which ignore risks of higher future costs.

A third of all disabled people already live in poverty but the Bill will now enforce destitution for some families and individual disabled people. The amendments would merely have softened the blow of the cumulative impact of the Government's cuts.

Neil Coyle adds:

'Disabled people remain the hardest hit by cuts. But the Government has completely failed to analyse the full cost of proposals. Cuts have consequences for disabled people and their families, but will also mean the NHS and councils experience higher costs through higher health, care and poverty needs. The Government has today chosen to ignore long-term needs and costs in the short-term search for departmental savings.'

2 February 2012

⇨ The above information is reprinted with kind permission from Disability Rights UK. Visit the Disability Alliance website at www.disabilityalliance.co.uk for more information on this and other related topics.

© *Disability Alliance*

UN NEWS CENTRE / DISABILITY ALLIANCE

Home care often fails to meet older people's basic rights, says inquiry

Information from the Equality and Human Rights Commission.

The Commission's inquiry into the home care system in England reveals disturbing evidence that the poor treatment of many older people is breaching their human rights and too many are struggling to voice their concerns about their care or be listened to about what kind of support they want.

The final report of the Commission's inquiry, *Close to home: older people and human rights in home care*, says hundreds of thousands[1] of older people lack protection under the Human Rights Act and calls for this legal loophole to be closed. It questions commissioning practices that focus on a rigid list of tasks, rather than what older people actually want, and that give more weight to cost than to an acceptable quality of care.

Around half of the older people, friends and family members who gave evidence to the inquiry expressed real satisfaction with their home care. They most valued having a small number of familiar and reliable staff who took the time to talk to them and complied with their requests to do specific tasks. Home care workers said their job satisfaction came from improving the quality of older people's lives.

But the inquiry also revealed many examples of older people's human rights being breached, including physical or financial abuse, disregarding their privacy and dignity, failing to support them with eating or drinking, treating them as if they were invisible, and paying little attention to what they want. Some were surprised that they had any choice at all as they thought they had little say in how their care was arranged.

For example, evidence given to the Commission included a woman being left stuck on the toilet in her bathroom, as the care worker said she was too busy completing the list of care tasks to help her; and people with dementia not being prompted to eat or their food 'hidden' in the fridge, so they go hungry; and a woman who asked for help with her washing up and to be assisted to walk out into her garden but was given help washing herself instead.

Ways for older people to complain about their home care are either insufficient or not working effectively. Reasons for their reluctance to make a complaint about their treatment included not wanting to get their care workers into trouble, fearing repercussions such as a worse standard of care or no care at all and preferring to make do rather than make a fuss.

The inquiry reveals the pervasive social isolation and loneliness experienced by many older people confined to their homes, who lack support to get out and take part in community life. Yet evidence from the home care industry indicates that social activities are some of the first support services to be withdrawn when local authorities cut back their spending on care services.

Alarmingly, one in three local authorities had already cut back on home care spending and a further one in five planned to do so within the next year.

The low rates that some local authorities pay for home care raises serious concerns about the pay and conditions of workers, including payment of the minimum wage. The low pay and status of care workers does not match the level of responsibility or the skills they need to provide quality home care. A high turnover of staff as a result of these factors has a negative impact on the quality of care given to older people.

The inquiry found age discrimination was a significant barrier to older people getting home care. It found that people over the age of 65 are getting less money towards their care than younger people with similar care needs, and are offered a more limited range of services in comparison. It also found that local authority phone contact lines can screen out older people needing home care without passing them on for a full assessment – which is unlawful.

Very few local authority contracts for home care specify that the provider must comply with the Human Rights Act. This undermines the quality of care that older people are getting. The evidence given to the inquiry indicates that where human rights are embedded into the way home care is provided – from commissioning to service delivery – high-quality care is delivered without necessarily increasing costs.

In response to the findings of its inquiry, the Commission says that legislation and regulation needs to be updated to reflect huge shifts in how care is provided[2]. Its recommendations from the inquiry fall under three broad categories:

Proper protection

Closing the loophole in the Human Rights Act which would give protection to the growing number of older people receiving home care from private and voluntary sector agencies. The law was changed in this way in 2008 to protect residents of care homes who are funded by the state.

Effective monitoring

The Government, Care Quality Commission and local authorities need to work together better to build human rights into home care and make sure that abuses are detected faster and dealt with more effectively.

Clear guidance

Clear and robust guidance on human rights is needed for councils so they can use the opportunities they have to promote and protect older people's human rights in commissioning; older people also need guidance to help them make choices about care and to explain how their human rights should be protected.

Sally Greengross, Commissioner for the Equality and Human Rights Commission, said:

'It is essential that care services respect people's basic human rights. This is not about burdensome red tape, it is about protecting people from the kind of dehumanising treatment we have uncovered. The emphasis is on saving pennies rather than providing a service which will meet the very real needs of our grandparents, our parents, and eventually all of us.

'This inquiry proposes some steps that would make sure human rights are protected in future – including changes to the law so that, at a minimum, all people getting publicly funded home care are protected by the Human Rights Act. Currently this is not the case.

'Most of us will want to carry on living in our own homes in later life, even if we need help to do so. When implemented, the recommendations from this inquiry will provide secure foundations for a home care system that will let us do so safely, with dignity and independence.'

Human rights in home care inquiry

The Commission's inquiry into the protection and promotion of human rights of older people in England who require or receive home-based care and support was launched in November 2010. The findings and recommendations have been drawn from a broad evidence base gathered from 1,254 individuals, local authorities, care providers and other organisations across England.

A copy of the report *Close to home: older people and human rights in home care* and an executive summary can be found at: www.equalityhumanrights.com/homecareinquiry

Human rights law in home care

The Human Rights Act states that public authorities must comply with the European Convention on Human Rights when they are carrying out their powers and duties. Centrally important for home care is the cluster of rights protected by Article 8 of the European Convention on Human Rights, which guarantees respect for dignity and personal autonomy, family life and social relationships. Other important rights include the prohibition on inhuman or degrading treatment (Article 3); and the right to life (Article 2).

Bare compliance with the Human Rights Act is not enough; public authorities also have 'positive obligations' to promote and protect human rights, meaning that they should take active steps to promote and protect human rights when they are carrying out their powers and duties. These positive human rights obligations are particularly important when local authorities are commissioning services from private and third sector organisations. As a result of court decisions, the legal safety net provided by the Human Rights Act does not extend to older people receiving home care from private and voluntary sector agencies. This legal loophole, combined with the shift away from local authorities delivering care themselves to commissioning it from external providers, means that the majority of older people using home care services have no direct human rights protection.

Equality and Human Rights Commission

The Commission is a statutory body established under the Equality Act 2006, which took over the responsibilities of the Commission for Racial Equality, the Disability Rights Commission and the Equal Opportunities Commission. It is the independent advocate for equality and human rights in Britain. It aims to reduce inequality, eliminate discrimination, strengthen good relations between people, and promote and protect human rights. The Commission enforces equality legislation on age, disability, gender reassignment, marriage and civil partnership, pregnancy and maternity, race, religion or belief, sex and sexual orientation, and encourages compliance with the Human Rights Act. It also gives advice and guidance to businesses, the voluntary and public sectors, and to individuals.

Notes

1   An estimated one in five (20 per cent) older people living at home receive care services. In 2009-10 about 453,000 people received home care through their local authority, excluding those in receipt of direct payments.

2   Since the Human Rights Act came into force in 2000, the home care industry has changed from having 56 per cent of care delivered by the private and voluntary sector to 84 per cent.

23 November 2011

⇨ Information from the Equality and Human Rights Commission. Visit www.equalityhumanrights.com for more information.

© *The copyright and all other intellectual property rights in* Home care often fails to meet older people's basic rights, says inquiry *are owned by, or licensed to, the Commission for Equality and Human Rights, known as the Equality and Human Rights Commission ('the EHRC')*

Prisoners' rights: Westminster clashes with Strasbourg

Information from YouGov.

By John Humphrys

Who should decide what rights we should have? And what should those rights be? Those are the two stark questions that divided opinion this week when the House of Commons clashed with the European Court of Human Rights over the answers. The British Government has been left with a delicate problem to solve and the way it does could have far-reaching implications for our relationship with Europe.

The specific issue of contention is whether prisoners in Britain should have the right to vote. Since Parliament passed the Forfeiture Act in 1870, prisoners, except those on remand or those imprisoned for default or contempt, have been denied the right to vote. But in 2005, the European Court of Human Rights in Strasbourg ruled that this breached human rights and ordered the British Government to bring in legislation to rectify the situation. It has until this August to do so.

> **Since Parliament passed the Forfeiture Act in 1870, prisoners, except those on remand or those imprisoned for default or contempt, have been denied the right to vote**

David Cameron has said that the very idea of giving prisoners the right to vote makes him feel physically sick, but he acknowledges that the British Government, like everyone else, is subject to the rule of law and must abide by the court's judgment. He knows, too, that if the Government ignores the court's rulings, it could open itself indefinitely to compensation claims from prisoners that could cost the taxpayer tens of millions of pounds.

It is up to the Government to decide the details of new legislation, and the Prime Minister's initial suggestion was that the right to vote should be restored, but only to prisoners serving four years or fewer.

But many MPs, especially in Mr Cameron's own Tory party, have felt affronted by the whole thing. They feel not only that it is simply wrong for prisoners to be allowed to vote but, even more, that it should be for the British

Parliament rather than a European court to decide. A cross-party backbench motion tabled by the former Tory Shadow Home Secretary, David Davis, and the former Labour Home Secretary, Jack Straw, proposed that Parliament should decide the issue and that the status quo should be maintained. On Thursday, the House of Commons voted on the motion. Both frontbenches abstained and it was passed by 234 to 22.

The vote was not binding on the Government, but the latter now has the delicate job of finding a way to satisfy both Westminster and Strasbourg.

The issue of prisoners' votes itself is fairly simple. David Davis put the case against the right to vote. He said: 'The general point is very clear in this country – that is, that it takes a pretty serious crime to get yourself sent to prison. And as a result you have broken the contract with society to such a serious extent that you have lost all of those rights – your liberty and your right to vote.'

The more liberal view is that loss of freedom is sufficient punishment. Juliet Lyon of the Prison Reform Trust has said 'the nineteenth-century punishment of civic death' is excessive. Other reformers see the right to vote as part of the process of rehabilitation, of preventing prisoners from feeling wholly alienated from the society to which they will return. And others say the whole thing is academic: most prisoners wouldn't be bothered to vote anyway.

The constitutional issue of who should decide this issue is altogether more thorny. The obvious answer is Parliament. But it was a British government, with the authority of Parliament, which signed up to the European Convention of Human Rights. The Convention, the brainchild of Winston Churchill, was intended to defend human rights that had been so abused in the period up to and during the Second World War. The court in Strasbourg was established to protect those rights.

Critics of the Strasbourg court accuse of it being expansionist and of passing judgements far beyond the narrower notions of what constituted human rights back in the 1940s

The Convention is quite separate from the European Union and has its own debating forum in the Council of Europe. British people have been able to take cases of alleged human rights breaches to Strasbourg since long before Britain joined the EU, and the last Labour Government made it possible, through the Human Rights Act, for cases under the Convention to be heard in British courts. Being a signatory to the Convention, though, is regarded as a sort of certificate of democratic *bona fides* necessary to belong to the EU.

Critics of the Strasbourg court accuse of it being expansionist and of passing judgements far beyond the narrower notions of what constituted human rights back in the 1940s. In doing so, it's argued, the court has encroached on the ability of democratically elected parliaments to decide issues for themselves. In the Commons on Thursday, Jack Straw accused it of 'judicial activism', a charge that has also been levelled against Strasbourg by the former law lord, Lord Hoffman.

Defenders of the court say that, at least in the case of prisoners' voting rights, it was only because the British Parliament had not been doing its own job properly that the court found itself having to act. Parliament hadn't bothered to debate the issue since 1870 so, when prisoners complained, it was only right that someone took a look at the issue again.

What's your view?

⇨ Should prisoners be given the right to vote or not?

⇨ Do you think it is legitimate or not to regard voting as a human right, irrespective of whether or not the voter is a convicted criminal?

⇨ Do you think it is the sort of issue that the European Court of Human Rights should be considering or not?

⇨ Should the British Government be prepared to defy the ECHR even if it means paying out millions of pounds in compensation to prisoners?

⇨ Should the British Government pull out of the European Convention on Human Rights altogether?

⇨ If not, how do you think the British Government should square the circle and satisfy both Strasbourg and Westminster?

But those alarmed by what they regard as Strasbourg's sprawling jurisdiction see in the prisoners' votes case a chance to fight back. Blair Gibbs, of the think tank Policy Exchange, said: 'Now is the opportunity to go to the root of this problem which is the expansionist Strasbourg court. The UK Government should use prisoner votes to reassert its authority over Strasbourg and, if necessary, prepare to leave the court's jurisdiction if it cannot be reformed.'

To others, however, it is only a court such as the ECHR rather than a parliament which offers people any real hope of having their rights defended. The Labour MP Denis MacShane said: 'I believe that peoples of other regions of the world – Africa, Asia, South America – would die to have an ECHR to tell their government what to do.'

The British Government shows no wish at all to listen to those who would like to see Britain pull out of Strasbourg altogether. It would complicate its relationships within the European Union far too much if it did so. So it needs to find a policy on votes for prisoners that will satisfy the court and its own backbenchers. Thursday's vote will strengthen its hand with the court but it may also embolden those who will have no truck with giving prisoners the vote and will simply not put up with a court, and a European court at that, telling the British Parliament what to do.

16 May 2011

⇨ The above information was reproduced with kind permission from YouGov. Visit www.yougov.com for further information.

© YouGov

The death penalty facts and figures

Information from Amnesty International.

Abolitionist and non-abolitionist countries

More than two-thirds of the world's countries have abolished the death penalty in law or practice.

⇨ 97 countries have abolished the death penalty for all crimes;

⇨ Eight countries have abolished the death penalty for all crimes except extraordinary crimes such as those committed in times of war;

⇨ 34 countries are *de facto* abolitionists: the death penalty is still provided for in legislation but no executions have been carried out for at least ten years.

Therefore, 139 countries have abolished the death penalty *de jure* or *de facto*. However, 58 countries and territories still uphold the death penalty and use this punishment. That said, 'only' 23 countries carried out executions in 2010.

More than two-thirds of the world's countries have abolished the death penalty in law or practice

Progress made towards world abolition of the death penalty

Since 1990, more than 57 countries have abolished capital punishment for all crimes: in Africa (recent examples include Gabon, Togo and Burundi); the Americas (Mexico, Paraguay and Argentina); Asia Pacific (the Philippines and Samoa, Kyrgyzstan and Uzbekistan); and Europe and the South Caucasus (Armenia, Bosnia-Herzegovina and Cyprus).

In the Americas, the USA was the only nation to carry out executions in 2010 and one State, Illinois, abolished the death penalty in March 2011. In sub-Saharan Africa four countries executed prisoners: Botswana, Equatorial Guinea, Somalia and Sudan. In Asia, there were no executions in Afghanistan, Indonesia, Mongolia and Pakistan for the second year in a row. In Europe, only Belarus continues to use the death penalty and executed two prisoners in March 2010.

Death sentences and executions

During 2010, at least 527 prisoners (excluding China) were executed in 18 countries and at least 2,024 people were sentenced to death in 67 countries. These figures only reflect cases of which Amnesty International was aware and the actual number is certainly higher.

In 2010, the nations with the highest number of executions were China, Iran, Iraq, North Korea, Saudi Arabia and the United States.

International human rights treaties forbid the use of capital punishment for all those under 18 at the time of the crime of which they are accused

China and North Korea

Amnesty International has not given any estimates on the number of executions in China. Official national statistics on the application of capital punishment remain a state secret. It is believed that thousands of executions have taken place in 2010. However, even under these conditions, a positive development is under way: in February 2011, the National People's Congress of China passed a law reducing the number of offences punishable by death from 68 to 55. Amnesty International received reports that at least 60 people were executed in North Korea in 2010. Executions are usually carried out in secret, but an increased number of executions were held in public to serve as an example to others.

Iran, Saudi Arabia and Yemen

According to the information gathered by Amnesty International, Iran executed at least 252 individuals in 2010. According to Iran Human Rights' annual report, at least 546 people were executed in 2010, 312 of which have been confirmed officially or unofficially by the Iranian authorities. In Yemen, at least 53 people were executed in 2010. Saudi Arabia executed at least 27 individuals, compared to 69 in 2009 and 102 in 2008.

United States of America

In the United States, 12 States carried out executions in 2010, taking the lives of 46 people (compared to 52 in 2009), therefore bringing the total number of people executed since capital punishment was reinstated in 1977 to 1,234. In March 2010, Illinois became the sixteenth State to abolish the death penalty, closely following New Mexico in 2009 and New Jersey in 2007.

Methods of execution

Since 2000 the following methods have been used:

⇨ decapitation (Saudi Arabia);

- ⇨ electrocution (United States);

- ⇨ hanging (Egypt, Iran, Iraq, Japan, Jordan, Pakistan, Singapore…);

- ⇨ lethal injection (China, United States, Guatemala, Thailand);

- ⇨ execution by firing squad (Belarus, China, Somalia, Vietnam…);

- ⇨ stoning (Afghanistan, Iran).

Use of the death penalty against juvenile offenders

International human rights treaties forbid the use of capital punishment for all those under 18 at the time of the crime of which they are accused. This ban is inscribed in the International Covenant on Civil and Political Rights, the American Convention on Human Rights and the Convention on the Rights of the Child.

The countries which still uphold capital punishment for some crimes are all party to at least one of these treaties which expressly forbid the execution of juvenile offenders. However, a small number of countries continue to execute juvenile offenders.

In 2010, Iran, Pakistan, Saudi Arabia, Sudan, United Arab Emirates and Yemen imposed death sentences on individuals that were below 18 years of age when the crimes were committed. In Nigeria, although Nigeria's Child Rights Act prohibits the death penalty, more than 20 prisoners currently on death row were sentenced for offences committed when they were below the age of 18.

International instruments supporting abolition

One important aspect of the progress which has been made recently is the adoption of international treaties through which States pledge not to use capital punishment:

- ⇨ Second Optional Protocol to the International Covenant on Civil and Political Rights, which aims to abolish the death penalty and has been ratified by 73 States. Three other countries have signed the Protocol, thereby signalling their intention to become party to this instrument at a later date;

- ⇨ Protocol to the American Convention on Human Rights on the abolition of the death penalty has been ratified by 11 States on the American continent;

- ⇨ Protocol No. 6 to the Convention for the Protection of Human Rights and Fundamental Freedoms (European Human Rights Convention) on the abolition of the death penalty, which has been ratified by 46 European States and signed by one other;

- ⇨ Protocol No. 13 to the European Human Rights Convention concerning the abolition of the death penalty in all circumstances, which has been ratified by 42 European States and signed by three others.

The object of Protocol No. 6 to the European Human Rights Convention is the abolition of the death penalty in peace time whereas Protocol No. 13 provides for the total abolition of the death penalty in all circumstances.

The two other protocols provide for the total abolition of capital punishment but give States the possibility, if they so wish, to use it exceptionally in times of war.

- ⇨ The above information is reproduced with kind permission from Amnesty International. Visit www.amnesty.org for further information.

© Amnesty International 2011

JUSTICE?

Death penalty abolition

Death penalty as inhuman and degrading treatment: case studies from the European Court of Human Rights.

Death row

Soering vs UK (application no. 14038/88) 7 July 1989

Mr Jens Soering was a German national detained in a prison in England pending extradition to the United States of America (USA) to face charges of murder for the stabbing to death of his girlfriend's parents. He complained that, notwithstanding the assurances presented to the UK Government, there was a serious likelihood that he would be sentenced to death if extradited to the USA. He maintained that, in particular because of the 'death row phenomenon' where people spent several years in extreme stress and psychological trauma waiting to be executed, if extradited he would be subjected to inhuman and degrading treatment and punishment contrary to Article 3 of the European Convention on Human Rights.

The European Court of Human Rights found that Mr Soering's extradition to the USA would expose him to a real risk of treatment contrary to Article 3. In reaching that conclusion, the Court had regard to the very long period of time people usually spent on death row in extreme conditions in the USA with an ever-mounting anguish of waiting to be executed, as well as to the personal circumstances of Mr Soering, especially his age and mental state at the time of the offence. The Court also noted that the legitimate purpose of the extradition could be achieved by another means which would not involve suffering of such exceptional intensity or duration. Accordingly, the UK decision to extradite Mr Soering to the USA would, if implemented, breach Article 3.

Risk of being sentenced to death

Bader and Kanbor vs Sweden (application no. 13284/04) 8 November 2005

The applicants were a family of four Syrian nationals who had had their asylum applications refused in Sweden and deportation orders to be returned to Syria served on them. They complained that as the father in the family had been convicted in his absence of complicity in a murder and sentenced to death in Syria, he ran a real risk of being executed if returned there.

The Court considered that Mr Bader had a justified and well-founded fear that the death sentence against him would be executed if he was forced to return to his home country. Since executions were carried out without any public scrutiny or accountability, the circumstances surrounding it would inevitably cause him considerable fear and anguish. As regards the criminal proceedings which had led to the death sentence, the Court found that, because of their summary nature and the total disregard of the rights of the defence, they had been a flagrant denial of a fair trial. The Court concluded that the death sentence imposed on Mr Bader following an unfair trial would cause him and his family additional fear and anguish as to their future if they were forced to return to Syria. Accordingly, the applicants' deportation to Syria, if implemented, would give rise to violations of Articles 2 and 3.

Death penalty as such contrary to the Convention

Al-Saadoon and Mufdhi vs UK (application no. 61498/08) 2 March 2010

The case concerned the complaint by the applicants, both Iraqi nationals and Sunni Muslims accused of involvement in the murder of two British soldiers shortly after the invasion of Iraq in 2003, that their transfer by the British authorities into Iraqi custody put them at real risk of execution by hanging.

The Court emphasised that although 60 years ago, when the Convention was drafted, the death penalty had not violated international standards, there had been a subsequent evolution towards its complete abolition, in law and in practice, within all 47 Council of Europe/Convention Member States. Two Protocols to the Convention had entered into force, abolishing the death penalty in time of peace (Protocol No. 6) and in all circumstances (Protocol No. 13), and the UK had ratified them both. All but two Convention States had signed Protocol 13 and all but three States which had signed it had ratified it. That demonstrated that Article 2 had been amended so as to prohibit the death penalty in all circumstances. Consequently, the Court held that the death penalty, which involved the deliberate and premeditated destruction of a human being by the State authorities causing physical pain and intense psychological suffering as a result of the foreknowledge of death, could be considered inhuman and degrading and, as such, contrary to Article 3 of the Convention.

October 2011

⇨ Information from the European Court of Human Rights. Visit www.echr.coe.int for further information on this and other related topics. This factsheet does not bind the Court and is not exhaustive.

© European Court of Human Rights 2011

⇨ Since 2007, the Government has been investigating whether the Human Rights Act should be replaced by a British Bill of Rights. Some argue that, because of its tie to Europe, the Human Rights Act does not sufficiently protect the rights of British citizens. (page 7)

⇨ 48% of the world now poses 'extreme' or 'high' risks of corporate complicity in human rights violations. (page 11)

⇨ Russia, China, India and East Africa have the highest rates of human rights abuses, being classed as 'extreme' by the Maplecroft *Human Rights Atlas*. (page 12)

⇨ As many UK high street retailers continue to post increased profits, the real value of wages being paid to the millions of women and men employed in the industry is falling. (page 13)

⇨ The International Labour Organization (ILO) is the body of the United Nations which oversees labour issues. They are based in Geneva, Switzerland, and have representatives from 18 countries. (page 14)

⇨ The ILO estimates that more than 200 million children aged five to 17 are doing work that is damaging to their mental, physical and emotional development. (page 15)

⇨ There is concern amongst some organisations that the 2012 London Olympic Games will lead to an increase in sex trafficking in the UK. (page 20)

⇨ Europe and Africa have the highest rates of human trafficking victims, with nearly 10,000 identified in 2010. (page 21)

⇨ 46% of British people think that there are some instances in which British security services could be justified in using information from other countries that has been obtained through the use of torture. (page 22)

⇨ The United Nations Convention on the Rights of the Child was adopted in 1989. All of the countries in the world have now signed up to it except for Somalia and the United States of America. (page 24)

⇨ Around 4,000 children die every day from diarrhoea because they do not have access to clean drinking water. (page 24)

⇨ Enrolment in primary education in developing countries increased from 83 per cent in 2000 to 89 per cent in 2008. However, the current rate of progress means that the target set by the UN in their Millennium Development Goals will not be met by 2015. (page 27)

⇨ About 69 million school-age children are not in school. Almost half of them (31 million) are in sub-Saharan Africa, and more than a quarter (18 million) are in Southern Asia. (page 27)

⇨ Ethiopia and Guinea-Bissau have the highest child labour rates, with over 50% of children aged 5-14 engaged in child labour. (page 30)

⇨ Around the world people are killed or endure hate-motivated violence, torture, detention, criminalisation and discrimination in jobs, healthcare and education because of their real or perceived sexual orientation or gender identity. (page 31)

⇨ In 76 countries it is still illegal to engage in same-sex conduct. In at least five of these, it is punishable by death. (page 31)

⇨ 97 countries have abolished the death penalty for all crimes, eight countries have abolished the death penalty for all crimes except extraordinary crimes such as those committed in times of war and in 34 countries the death penalty is still provided for in legislation but no executions have been carried out in at least ten years. (page 37)

⇨ International human rights treaties forbid the use of capital punishment for those under 18 at the time of the crime of which they are accused. However, a small number of countries still execute juvenile offenders. (page 38)

European Convention on Human Rights

The European Convention on Human Rights was adopted by the Council of Europe in 1950 to enshrine the articles of the Universal Declaration of Human Rights, a declaration drafted in the aftermath of the Second World War in response to the atrocities of the Holocaust. The UK signed up to the Convention in 1951.

Human rights

The basic rights all human beings are entitled to, regardless of who they are, where they live or what they do. Concepts of human rights have been present throughout history, but our modern understanding of the term emerged as a response to the horrific events of the Holocaust. While some human rights, such as the right not to be tortured, are absolute, others can be limited in certain circumstances: for example, someone can have their right to free expression limited if it is found they are guilty of inciting racial hatred.

The Human Rights Act

The Human Rights Act is a written law (statute) passed in 1998 which is in force in England and Wales. The rights that are protected by this law are based on the articles of the European Convention on Human Rights. There is an ongoing debate between supporters of the Act and its critics as to whether it should be kept, or replaced with a new UK Bill of Rights.

Millennium Development Goals

The Millennium Development Goals are made up of eight goals agreed upon by 193 United Nations member states. The aim is to achieve these goals by the year 2015. The goals are:

⇨ eradicating extreme poverty and hunger;

⇨ achieving universal primary education;

⇨ promoting gender equality and empowering women;

⇨ reducing child mortality rates;

⇨ improving maternal health;

⇨ combating HIV/AIDS, malaria, and other diseases;

⇨ ensuring environmental sustainability; and

⇨ developing a global partnership for development.

Slavery

A slave is someone who is denied their freedom, forced to work without pay and considered to be literally someone else's property. Although slavery is officially banned internationally, there are an estimated 27 million slaves worldwide. Article 4 of the Universal Declaration of Human Rights states that 'No one shall be held in slavery or servitude; slavery and the slave trade shall be prohibited in all their forms.'

Torture

Intentionally causing a person physical or mental pain or suffering in order to obtain information or force them to make a confession. Under Article 5 of the Universal Declaration of Human Rights, 'No one shall be subjected to torture or to cruel, inhuman or degrading treatment or punishment.' The subject of torture, and whether it might be considered a necessary evil in the war against terror, has recently been the subject of controversy.

Trafficking

The transport and/or trade of people from one area to another, usually for the purpose of forcing them into labour or prostitution.

United Nations Convention on the Rights of the Child (UNCRC)

An international human rights treaty that protects the rights of all children and young people under 18. The UK signed the convention on 19 April 1990 and ratified it on 16 December 1991. When a country ratifies the convention it agrees to do everything it can to implement it. Every country in the world has signed the convention except the USA and Somalia.

Universal Declaration of Human Rights

The first international, secular agreement on what were formerly called 'the rights of man', which arose from the desire of the world's governments to prevent the recurrence of the atrocities of the Second World War by setting out a shared bill of rights for all peoples and all nations. The text is non-binding, but it retains its force as the primary authority on human rights, and has been supported by the UN's ongoing work to encourage its incorporation into domestic laws.

ACKNOWLEDGEMENTS

The publisher is grateful for permission to reproduce the following material.

While every care has been taken to trace and acknowledge copyright, the publisher tenders its apology for any accidental infringement or where copyright has proved untraceable. The publisher would be pleased to come to a suitable arrangement in any such case with the rightful owner.

Chapter One: Human Rights Issues

An introduction to human rights, © EHRC, *Human Rights Act myths,* © Liberty, *Should we repeal the Human Rights Act?,* © Total Politics, *UK bill of rights commission should open up,* © Guardian News & Media Ltd 2012, *New snooping powers could be illegal, human rights watchdog warns,* © Telegraph Media Group Limited 2012, *Global increase in human rights violations,* © Maplecroft, *Let's clean up fashion 2011,* © Labour Behind the Label, *All workers have rights,* © 2012 ICTU, *An overview of human trafficking,* © SOCA Serious Organised Crime Agency 2012, *Sex trafficking and prostitution,* © 2012 Anti-Trafficking Alliance, *UK complicity in torture,* © Liberty, *Obtained under torture,* © YouGov, *UK torture complicity inquiry 'scrapped',* © 2012 Press Association.

Chapter Two: Minority Rights

Issues surrounding children's rights, © 2011 UNICEF UK, *Millennium Development Goal 2: achieving universal primary education,* © Department of Public Information, United Nations, *UK 'lagging behind' on children's rights,* © 2012 Dods Parliamentary Communications Ltd, *UN issues first report on human rights of gay and lesbian people,* © UN News Centre, *Government rejects welfare amendments and ignores consequences of DLA cuts,* © Disability Alliance, *Home care often fails to meet older people's basic rights, says inquiry,* © EHRC, *Prisoner's rights: Westminster clashes with Strasbourg,* © YouGov, *The death penalty facts and figures,* © Amnesty International 2011, *Death penalty abolition,* © European Court of Human Rights 2011.

Illustrations

Pages 1, 18, 22, 29: Angelo Madrid; pages 2, 13, 25, 35: Don Hatcher; pages 7, 19, 28, 38: Simon Kneebone; pages 14, 21: Bev Aisbett.

Cover photography

Left: © Miguel Ugalde. Centre: © Margarita Rodríguez Queiruga. Right: © Ramzi Hashisho.

Additional acknowledgements

Editorial on behalf of Independence Educational Publishers by Cara Acred.

With thanks to the Independence team: Mary Chapman, Sandra Dennis and Jan Sunderland.

Lisa Firth
Cambridge
April, 2012

ASSIGNMENTS

The following tasks aim to help you think through the debate surrounding human rights and provide a better understanding of the topic.

1 Design a booklet to explain the content and scope of the Human Rights Act 1998. Include a timeline demonstrating its history and its links to the Universal Declaration of Human Rights. Consider who the Act protects, and how it is enforced. Use the Internet and newspapers to find some examples of the Human Rights Act being enforced in the UK and include at least two of these in your booklet.

2 Since 2007, the Government has been investigating the possibility of replacing the Human Rights Act with a British Bill of Rights. Read *Should we repeal the Human Rights Act?* on pages 7-8. Use the Internet to do some further research and then write an objective article summarising the arguments for and against a British Bill of Rights. When you have done this, conduct a survey to find out whether people in your class would support or oppose the new Bill. Present your findings in a pie chart alongside your article.

3 Write your own Bill of Rights for the UK. What rights do you think should be enshrined in law? Would all rights be absolute, or could some be limited in certain circumstances? What stipulations and provisos would you want to include with your list of rights?

4 Read *Let's clean up fashion 2011* on page 13. Imagine that you are one of the workers from Cambodia who went on strike to ask for a minimum wage of $93 per month. Write a diary entry describing a typical working day on a sub-living wage. You may want to do some research beforehand on living costs in Cambodia, to get an idea of the quality of life someone would have earning only the average textile worker's salary.

5 'This house believes that in certain circumstances, it is both acceptable and necessary for UK courts to consider evidence gained under torture in other states.' Read *UK complicity in torture* and *Obtained under torture* on pages 19-22 then debate this motion as a class, with one half arguing in favour and the other against.

6 Read the book 'Nineteen Eighty-Four' by George Orwell, set in a future dystopia in which the right to free expression is controlled by the nightmarish 'Big Brother'. Write a review. Do you think Orwell saw his book as a warning? If you wish to take this activity further you could go on to plan and write your own short story, set in a future world where human rights are either limited or greatly extended. How would this affect people's lives?

7 Design a poster illustrating children's rights as enshrined in the UN Convention on the Rights of the Child. Include at least five of the articles defined by the Convention.

8 Find out about the Smith case mentioned in the EHRC article *An introduction to human rights on* pages 1-3. Write a summary of the case and why it is relevant to the human rights debate.

9 Look at the 'Human Rights Risk Atlas' map on page 12. Label as many countries on the map as you can. Choose one of the countries categorised as being at extreme, high or medium risk and do some research into human rights violations in this region. Create a Powerpoint presentation about the plight of people in this region and present it to your class.

10 Read the diary of a former slave in the United States, such as Frederick Douglass (published 1845) or Harriet Jacobs (published 1861). What human rights were Douglass and Jacobs deprived of? As a modern reader, do you find their accounts shocking?

11 Imagine you are a lawyer appearing in court to argue that the Government's reform of Disability Living Allowance constitutes a breach of disabled people's human rights. Using your knowledge of the Human Rights Act, draft your argument and present this to your class.

12 Read Harper Lee's 'To Kill a Mockingbird'. How and why is the character of Tom Robinson denied his basic human rights? Write an essay exploring your feelings.

13 Prepare a talk for your class explaining why human rights are important. Consider both UK and global human rights issues. Prepare a handout with key facts to accompany your presentation.

14 Do you support or oppose the so-called 'ticking time bomb scenario', which is sometimes cited as a justification for the use of torture? Is this a valid scenario, or simply a 'strawman' created by torture apologists? Write an essay exploring the arguments for and against this justification and giving your own conclusion.